GW00992258

Seasons of Hope

www.**transworldbooks**.co.uk

www.transworldireland.ie

Seasons of Hope

Sister Stan

Be kind whenever possible. It is always possible.

HH THE DALAI LAMA

TRANSWORLD IRELAND

TRANSWORLD IRELAND
an imprint of The Random House Group Limited
20 Vauxhall Bridge Road, London SW1V 2SA
www.transworldbooks.co.uk

First published in 2014 by Transworld Ireland,
a division of Transworld Publishers

A CIP catalogue record for this book
is available from the British Library.

ISBN 9781848272118

Addresses for Random House Group Ltd companies outside the UK
can be found at: www.randomhouse.co.uk
The Random House Group Ltd Reg. No. 954009

The Random House Group Limited supports the Forest Stewardship Council®
(FSC®), the leading international forest-certification organisation. Our books car-
rying the FSC label are printed on FSC®-certified paper. FSC is the only
forest-certification scheme supported by the leading environmental organisations,
including Greenpeace. Our paper procurement policy can be found at
www.randomhouse.co.uk/environment

Typeset in Berkeley Old Style 10.5/15pt by Falcon Oast Graphic Art Ltd.
Printed and bound in Great Britain by
Clays Limited, Bungay, Suffolk

2 4 6 8 10 9 7 5 3 1

For Josie O'Rourke –
her love of all beings, especially animals,
inspires me every day

Essays and Poetry Contributions

'The Promised Garden' (poem) Theo Dorgan   1

'A New Story to Guide Us' by Seán McDonagh   14

'The Magic of Meditation' by Ruairí
  McKiernan   43

'The Gift of Life' by Síle Wall   72

'Legends' (poem) Eavan Boland   84

'A Soul for Society' by Sister Thérèse   106

'Meditation' by Korko Moses, SJ   148

'Why We Need a Spirituality' by Peter McVerry   193

'The Meditation Session' by Michael Harding   230

'This Moment' (poem) Eavan Boland   251

Introduction

The layout of this book is like poetry, but this was never meant to be poetry; I'm only trying to use my thoughts and words to open our hearts and minds, to realize that all our lives are fleeting moments in which are found the seeds of peace, unity, stillness and love. I offer them as a support and enhancement of the spirituality of those who are seeking stillness in their lives and I leave whatever needs to be revealed to the divine wisdom within.

The seven beautiful essays included here enrich the book with great insights. I am grateful to Michael Harding, Seán McDonagh, Thérèse Murphy, Ruairí McKiernan, Peter McVerry, Korko Moses and Síle Wall for their great generosity in contributing pieces that I know you, the readers, will enjoy and appreciate. I would like to thank Eavan Boland

and Theo Dorgan who kindly gave me permission to use their inspirational poems, 'This Moment' and 'The Promised Garden' respectively. I am grateful to Treasa Coady and Siobhan Parkinson for their encouragement and advice. A special thanks to my editor Brenda Kimber at Transworld for her assistance, support, advice and help in bringing this book to completion. Big thanks also to Johanne Farrelly who typed several drafts of the book, and finally I want to thank all those people who have been part of my life and who are in this book in one way or another.

Sister Stan, 2014

The Promised Garden

There is a garden where our hearts converse,
at ease beside clear water, dreaming
a whole and perfect future for yourself,
myself, our children and our friends.

And if we must rise and leave,
put on identity and fight,
each day more desperate than the last
and further from our future, that
is no more than honour and respect shown
to all blocked from the garden that we own.

There is a garden at the heart of things,
our oldest memory guards it with her strong will.
Those who by love and work attain there
bathe in her living waters, lift up their hearts and
turn again to share the steep privations of the hill;
they walk in the market but their feet are still.

There is a garden where our hearts converse,
at ease beside clear water, dreaming
a whole and perfect future for yourself,
myself, our children and our friends.

Theo Dorgan

Prayer

The way
of the heart
inward
to the eternal truth
I am

The way of
freedom
accepting
trusting

The way of
offering
mind and heart
body and breath
bones and blood
head hands and feet

The way of
waiting
listening
holding
hearing
knowing
emptiness
fullness

The way of
silence
stillness
presence
quiet

The way of
opening and allowing
union
oneness
being
the sacred and the holy

This Day

Alive

Awake

Now

Fully aware

attentive

face to face with what is

touching the infinity in the now

open to the mystery of being

Living Each Moment

Present moment

only moment

the future of

the entire

cosmos

depending on

how I live

this moment in time

There exists only the present instant . . .
a Now which always and without end is
itself new. There is no yesterday nor any
tomorrow, but only Now, as it was a
thousand years ago and as it will be a
thousand years hence.

MEISTER ECKHART

Gratitude

All is gift
every moment
every breath
every move
this moment
this alive moment
all is gift

Gratitude
a way of being
we become it
it becomes us

The word
became flesh
to teach
gratitude

Hope

Standing on the edge
of new beginnings
of unknown futures
on the threshold of what
has yet to be born.

This new moment
pregnant with promise
open to
unimagined possibilities
without certainty
or security
trusting what
is not yet

The Call

The call
comes from the margins
not the centre
from the desert
not the chapel

An unexplored destination
places unknown
no path
only moments revealed
in the throbbing of pain
and the voices of suffering

The call
urging and impelling us on

Vision

Seeing, with new eyes,
seeing clearly the depth of what is.
Seeing to the horizons
receding
believing in destinations beyond
journeying to the edge
of the edge
allowing the
yet to be
discovered road
to lead us

Attachment

Attached to a genuine good
ensnared
until the link
however delicate
is broken
Free
to live fully
to fall into the arms
of the love that awaits us
To discover the one ultimate good

Spring

seeds stirring
sounding
crackling
sprouting

Grass rising
from the dark stony brown earth
colouring the hills and valleys
with myriad shades of green

Closeted bulbs burst open
their strong protective coats
Shrubs and trees bud forth
to their delicately forming leaves
An abundance of weeds
and garden pests emerge
finding a new foothold
in the warming earth

Resurrection

Birdsong and call echo and re-echo
across the land
marking the beginning of mating and nesting
Melted snow and thawed water
release fish
to move and swim and spawn again

A surge of life explodes over the whole earth
each day something new

Don't judge each day by the harvest you reap but by the seeds that you plant.

ROBERT LOUIS STEVENSON

A New Story to Guide Us

Fr. Seán McDonagh, SSC

More Christians across the world celebrate the Feast of Christmas than Easter, even though liturgically speaking Easter, which celebrates the Resurrection of Christ, is the high point of the Church's celebrations each year. Even here there is a bit of an anomaly; more people attend the Good Friday liturgy than the Easter Vigil. The Vigil begins with the lighting of the Paschal Candle, a symbol of the Risen Christ as the 'Light of the World'. Following the singing of the *Exultet* (The Song of Gratitude), the Liturgy of the Word begins. The first reading, from Genesis 1: 1–2.4a, takes us back to the very beginning of creation and presents its unfolding from 'Let there be light' through the creation of humans – 'let us make man in our own image and likeness', to the creation of the Sabbath: 'on the seventh day God completed the work he had been doing' (Gen. 2: 1–2).

I am lucky to have studied the Bible in the mid-1960s when the Catholic Church had finally accepted the insights of modern biblical scholarship. We learned about the importance of the above text in liturgical celebrations; the equality of women and men, even in a decidedly patriarchal society, and the importance of coming together each Sabbath to retell the stories about God's goodness to the people of Israel.

It was only when I began working with the T'boli, a tribal people who lived in the hills of South Cotabato in the Philippines, that I began to see how a powerful myth could give meaning to people's lives and guide their behaviour. Because of their isolation in the tropical forests, the T'bolis had little contact with the Spanish regime that ruled the Philippines from 1565 to 1998; nor, later, were they influenced by Islam. The T'boli had a wonderfully rich and complex culture. Their myth of origin was built around their mythical founder, Tudbulul. During festivals such as the Mo Nimum (a celebration of fertility and marriage) T'boli singers would sing and chant about the activities of Tudbulul. This story gave them an identity, and told them how they should interact with other T'boli, with nearby tribes, and with the natural world. As my competence in the language improved, I marvelled at how young and old would listen spellbound as a singer recounted the heroic deeds of Tudbulul.

This led us at the Santa Cruz Mission in the T'boli hills to include a part of the Tudbulul myth in readings at the Easter Vigil. This, in turn, brought me to reflect on the impact of Genesis on me, the first time I heard it. For me it was not a myth or guiding story as that of Tudbulul was for the majority of T'bolis, yet for over a thousand years this account of the universe's creation by a loving God did serve as a myth of origin for Europeans. Unlike other cosmologies in the Middle East, which maintained that there were two equally powerful forces, of good and evil, Genesis affirms that the world and all its creatures are good. Genesis opposed cosmologies such as Manichaenism which viewed the world as evil.

In Genesis there is no evolutionary unfolding: each species is created directly by God. The Great Chain of Being runs from very simple life forms to the creation of humans at the top point of the pyramid. Everything in the world existed primarily for humans: 'Be fruitful, multiply, fill the earth and conquer it' (Gen. 1: 28). Other species had no intrinsic value. The Earth was the centre of the cosmos and the world was relatively young. In 1650, the Church of Ireland Archbishop of Armagh, James Ussher, following careful calculations, claimed that the world began on Sunday, 23 October 4004 BC.

The first crack in this edifice came with the publication of Copernicus's *De revolutionibus orbium coelestium* (On the Revolutions of the Celestial Spheres), just before his death in 1543. This challenged the theory of Aristotle and Ptolemy that the Earth was the centre of the universe. For Copernicus the Sun was the centre of the solar system. Interestingly enough, it was not until this view was espoused by Galileo in 1610 that it drew critical comments from the Catholic Church authorities, resulting in the condemnation of Galileo's *Dialogue Concerning the Two Chief World Systems* by the Inquisition in 1633.

In the seventeenth century, the focus of scientific endeavour moved from astronomy to geology. The Danish geologist and anatomist Nicolaus Steno studied the strata and fossils of Tuscany and developed geological theories of how landscapes were formed. If rock strata are formed by sedimentary deposits then the world is more than 6,000 years old. Steno was the first to recognize that fossils are the remains of living creatures, and therefore that the world could not have been created in just a few days, as would be assumed by an uncritical reading of Genesis. The questions that the fossil record raises for the emergence of life was taken up by botanists such as Buffon and Lamarck in the eighteenth century. Lamarck's theories of evolution are in conflict with those of Charles Darwin, so less attention has been paid to his work. Yet he was one of the first scientists to relate fossil remains to the living organisms that they most closely resemble in today's world.

Darwin revolutionized biology with his publication of *The Origin of Species* (1859) and *The Descent of Man* (1871). When he set out on his travels on the *Beagle* in 1831, he held the widespread belief that species were immutable. As he journeyed around the world during the next five years studying plants, animals, birds and their habitats, he began to question the accepted doctrine on creation. In the Galapagos Islands, west of Ecuador, he found similar but distinct flora and fauna on adjacent islands and realized that these closely related species had developed from a common ancestor rather than through separate creations by God. It took another twenty-three years of study before he felt free to publish the results of his research. The book, which drew fire from many quarters, was the final nail in the coffin of the traditional worldview.

But just as the old cosmology was disintegrating, a new cosmology, built on the foundations of modern science, began to appear. Modern cosmology, particularly the research of a Belgian Catholic priest Georges Lemaître (1894–1966), continuing the work of Albert Einstein, posits that the universe began 13.7 billion years ago. This moment of origin of everything in the universe was referred to in a disparaging way as the 'Big Bang' by Fred Hoyle, the mathematician and astronomer, who had been one of the leading proponents of the steady-state model which was then the generally accepted cosmology. Lemaître's emerging universe tells us that all that exists today can be traced back through millions of transformations to that sacred moment. For over 100,000 years, matter, as we know it, did not appear. As the universe expanded and simultaneously cooled, protons and neutrons fused into atomic nuclei to form the hydrogen atom. Gradually the galaxies formed as enormous clouds coalesced into stars under the pressure of gravity. As the temperature rose, nuclear fires ignited at the core of these giant stars, transforming nitrogen into helium. The collapse of these supernovas then created heavy elements such as carbon, iron, phosphorus and sulphur – essential atoms in every living creature.

Our solar system was originally a diffuse cloud of cosmic dust and gas from debris spewed across the sky by the supernova explosions. Eventually, our Earth was born. It went through extraordinary transformations, until about 3.8 billion years ago when the perfect conditions for the next breakthrough in creation arose. This is the emergence of life. We do not know how a self-replicating, information-carrying molecule assembled spontaneously from compounds such as amino acids, but this cell, with its membrane to absorb nutrients and its ability to excrete waste and reproduce, became essential to all subsequent life forms, including human beings. One of these cells learned how to capture packets of energy coming from the sun and transform them into food, in the process releasing oxygen into the atmosphere. This wonderful technology, on which all creatures which need oxygen depend, is called photosynthesis.

With the arrival of sexual reproduction about a billion years ago, life became much more complex and diverse. Various forms emerged – invertebrates, vertebrates, reptiles and mammals. About 600 million years ago life invaded land, initially in the form of plants. For 160 million years dinosaurs ruled the world until they were wiped out by a massive extinction 65 million years ago. With a dominant predator no longer on the scene, mammals could develop and colonize habitats across the globe. For the past 65 million years, known as the Cenozoic (new life) period, life on Earth has flourished with birds, flowering species, mammals, primates and finally humans. All parts of the living world are biologically and genetically connected. Humans share 98.4 per cent of orang-utans' genes – and 36 per cent of fruit flies'.

About two million years ago in Africa, humans emerged, then *Homo sapiens* about 70,000 years ago, at the height of the last Ice Age. Because sea levels were 60 metres lower than today humans easily moved south across India and South East Asia and reached Australia about 60,000 years ago. Humans also colonized East Asia and moved across the Bering Strait about 22,000 years ago to the Americas. Originally, these small groups of hunters and gatherers made very little impact on their wider environment. This changed quite significantly with the introduction of farming 10,000 years ago. The domestication of plants and animals, which provided a more secure food supply, caused human settlements to grow in size: a thousand or more people could be found in a Neolithic village. Five thousand years ago classical civilizations emerged in the Middle East, then in China, modern-day Pakistan and still later in Central and South America. New forms of government and ritual practices arose, reflecting the different tasks required in a more developed society. Armies were formed and greater conflicts fought. The gap between rich and poor widened and humans began to exploit and often enslave other human beings.

A new phase of human impact on the planet began in the seventeenth century, with the emergence of the scientific era. Humans learned an enormous amount about the emergence of the universe and planet Earth. Many technologies of this time have brought improvements in living conditions for people in economically rich countries and for the élite in the poor countries. However, the impact of some technologies on the integrated functioning of the planet has often been negative. Burning fossil fuel for the past two hundred years has changed the chemistry of our planet and threatens to bring about changes of a geological order of magnitude unless we urgently reduce carbon emissions into the atmosphere. The demands that humans make on global habitats are threatening to bring about the sixth-largest extinction of life since life began 3.8 billion years ago. We are poisoning the oceans and destroying ecosystems such as coral reefs and mangrove forests. We forget that the oceans are the cradle of life.

It is essential to remember that our actions always end by having an impact on real places and situations, from the tropical forests of the T'boli hills to the pasture lands and rivers of County Meath in Ireland. There is a new cosmology that tells us we are connected with every other reality on the planet and in the universe. Biologically and genetically, we are related to every known species. It challenges us to abandon our predatory approach and to develop sustainable ways of living. Instead of destroying ecosystems, this story can become a guiding myth, telling us who we are, and it can also act as a moral compass to guide us in our journey to a sustainable future. A liturgical version of this new cosmology has become part of our Easter Vigil liturgy. It provides the larger context for both the reading from Genesis and the myth of Tudbulul. I believe it should be part of every Easter Vigil liturgy across the globe – if possible, accompanied by a short PowerPoint presentation of photos from the Hubble telescope and from the local environment. Such a liturgical experience would energize Christians to dedicate themselves to protecting and enhancing God's creation.

Stopping

A time to stop
to sit
to be still
to wonder
to tune into a new beauty
in our lives
to discover again
the joy of a grateful heart
to begin again
ALLELUIA

Winter

Silence, stillness
no visible sign of growth
colourless
greys and brown
no scent
no sign of life

Deep within
hidden stirrings
roots strengthening their hold
bulbs preparing to venture
into light

Winter calling us
to listen to its voice
attend to its wisdom
allowing its touch into
the stillness of our inner life
appreciating our inner strength
embracing the seeds of beauty
recognizing the busyness of our lives
where silence is a stranger

For, lo, the winter is past,
the rain is over and gone;
The flowers appear on the earth;
the time of the singing
of birds is come . . .

SONG OF SOLOMON CH. 2, V. 10

Be still and know what lies within

What lies above
below
behind
before
beside
around
outside me
is
limited
compared with
what lies within me
Goodness
love
peace
compassion
joy
forgiveness
gratitude
The infinite capacity
for union with

(Continued)

Brahman
Atman
Allah
Buddha
The universe
Holy Spirit

In Between

Dark becoming light
Night becoming day
Autumn becoming winter
Child becoming adult
Suffering becoming peace
Noise becoming silence
Life becoming death
One moment becoming the next moment
– elusive sacredness in time

Síle Wall

Transformation

Transformation
Unfolding in time
Unhurried
Moment by moment by moment
Slowing me down
to let go
to surrender

Teaching me Freedom
from the pressure to
achieve
create
to produce
to harvest

Inviting me to hear
the small beckoning voice
in the quiet space
of my inner self

Commuting

Early morning
traffic jams
stress
pressure
bored
worried
hassled
other cars
other people
bored
worried
hassled
coming into the present
looking beyond the exterior facade
to the changing sky
coming into the present
sending them blessings

Be Still

Be still my heart
Enter the great
sound of silence
within
of emptiness calling to fullness
overwhelming vastness
absolute stillness
total presence
unrestricted love –
no past
no future
only now
calling to deeper worlds
transforming me
within the great silence

Trust

Living into the
mystery of
God
Ourselves
Others
The universe
Life

Seeing without prejudice
Hearing without words
Living the questions with trust
Pregnant with promise
Opening the heart
to contagious possibilities
embracing risk
trusting what is not yet

Listening

Letting go of certainties
seeing anew
what we took for granted
discovering
what we are not looking for
finding extraordinary ways
to do ordinary things
aware of
God dreaming in us
for our world
no more war
violence
famine
or
want

To listen well, is as powerful a means of influence as to talk well, and is as essential to all true conversation.

<small>CHINESE PROVERB</small>

Mindful

Walking with awareness
enjoying each step
allowing people to pass me by
women with buggies
wheelchair users
older people carrying their daily shopping
children running
young people hurrying

Walking with awareness
enjoying each step
taking time to bid friends
and strangers the time of day
letting the street beggars know I care
assisting strangers with maps

Walking with awareness
enjoying each step

In the Moment

Breathing in the crisp clean air
staring into the starry sky
and blue red sunsets
marvelling at the early morning mist
silently evaporating
watching the frost melting
on the window ledge

Present Moment

In this present moment
In the now
Everything belongs
Past, present and future
This is my home
my life
Life is now
Only now

The Word

Attaching, linking, connecting
Today with yesterday
Tomorrow with today
Was there from the beginning

The Word
Shaping us into one
In freedom

Struggles, campaigns, causes
Prayer, reflections, words, letters
war, blood
tears, laughter
hatred, love
Humanity responding

Síle Wall

Be not afraid

Trusting something
new is happening
watching the new life
slowly rising within me

Trusting the miracle
of the new
transforming me
in ways that surprise
and amaze
filling me with hope
opening me to
the liberating power of God
leading to peace

Being Attentive

Mindfully living
in the present moment
seeing with the eyes
of the heart
to the core
beyond the senses
beneath the surface
to the sacredness of life
the dignity
and mysterious connectivity of all
bringing new possibilities
knowing there is no end

Trust

Our future lies
within our past
We step forward
by reaching back
grasped by what
we cannot understand
transforming us
into something
we already are

The Fisherman

Knows
Where and When and How
to catch and throw
and catch
and let go

Síle Wall

The Old Ash

I am old now
wiser than when I was planted
Many seasons lived through me
each spring a new unfolding
leaves one by one returning
Slowly I become a summer tree
my strong arms carrying the swing
small bare feet walking
in and out through me
looking for nests
With my hundreds of eyes
I watched transforming
circles of life
move through me
Crisp autumn breezes
caressing me
surrendering my leaves
to the bitter cold winds of winter
frost and snow and sleet
sweep through me and
sometimes cling to my naked body
and then new life buds through me again
weathering it all

For Mercy has a human heart
Pity a human face:
And Love, the human form divine,
And Peace, the human dress.

SONGS OF INNOCENCE, WILLIAM BLAKE

The Magic of Meditation

Ruairí McKiernan

Through the study of books one seeks God; by meditation one finds him.

PADRE PIO

My journey to meditation started in my mid-twenties. After years of travelling around the world, I found myself back in Ireland and feeling stressed by the huge challenges of setting up and running an organization. I realized I was living in my head, often concerned with the past or anxious about the future, and finding it difficult to be at peace in the present moment. Looking back, I feel I was half asleep and not living life to its full potential.

Illness and stress led me on a quest for well-being and to yoga and meditation. I decided that if I wanted to find peace, happiness and health, then it was up to me to take responsibility. It was the start of understanding that true happiness comes from within. I discovered that meditation helps me bring awareness to my thoughts, my relationships, my behaviour and my diet. It helps me tune in to my inner wisdom and make better decisions. It allows me to navigate the mental noise and filter through what's really important.

Meditation also gave me a freer way of looking at spirituality. It helped me to understand and to experience what God is and to see what is meant by the concept of Qi, or energy force. It gave me a sense of what the Holy Spirit might be. Meditation showed me what Einstein understood: that we are all divine parts of the interconnected web of life. It taught me that we don't need a middleman to know what the Native Americans call 'the great spirit'. Meditation is a tool for accessing truth, for waking up to reality, and for tasting true freedom.

The rising popularity of meditation and mindfulness is no accident. The fast pace of living and the emphasis on scientific, technological and material growth has ignored the need for inner connection. Increasingly people want to avoid stress and feel that there is more to life than a rat race of survival. Research shows that the average smartphone user checks their phone one hundred and fifty times a day. I love my phone and I love the internet but this isn't healthy. It's information overload. There is a fundamental disease at the heart of modern culture. The evidence is clear when you look at issues such as mental illness, obesity, addiction, and the disconnection from community and the natural world.

The ancient practice of meditation can open the door to a healthier relationship with oneself and with others. It can cultivate stillness. Different forms of meditation are practised in Hinduism, Islam, Judaism, Sikhism, Buddhism, Taoism and Christianity. Increasingly, it appeals to people who are seeking personal and spiritual growth outside religion.

Scientists, health professionals, educators, business leaders and sportspeople are catching on to the vast health benefits that meditation offers. Studies demonstrate that it can improve the immune system, ease pain, decrease inflammation, alleviate depression, stress and anxiety, cultivate compassion, improve emotional intelligence, and enhance memory, focus, attention and creativity. Meditation isn't a quick fix for health and happiness but in so many ways it is a wonder drug that the world can't afford to ignore. It's free, always accessible, and easy to learn.

When it comes to the practice of meditation, I'm still learning and always will be. My 'monkey mind' of compulsive thinking and its 50,000 daily thoughts doesn't give up easily. I know the only way to harness it is through practice. Meditation is like most things in that you get out of it what you put in. I like to think of it as basic mental hygiene, a daily ritual that declutters my mind. My meditation sittings can be as short as five minutes per day, although I often find ridiculous excuses to tell myself I still don't have time. I know this is because in many ways the busy mind, and the ego, will resist meditation because it fears it.

Once I went on a ten-day retreat where I hardly spoke to anyone. I was in a cabin by myself with no TV, phone or internet. My monkey mind didn't like the quiet at all and screamed 'Get out of here, you'll go mad!' Day three found me in an internet café trying to rearrange my flights to come home early. Thankfully I couldn't change the flights and by day four, and with the help of meditation, my mind gave up the fight and started to relax. By day six I was in bliss, at peace in the present moment. My mind had slowed right down. I got to connect with my intuition and process emotions, stresses and fears that needed my attention. I also slept a lot – something the Dalai Lama reckons can be the best meditation of all. When it was time for me to go home I didn't want to return to what seemed like the collective madness of the busy world.

Staying sane and calm among all the noise and stimulation is what encourages me to return to meditation. I mostly practise at home but sometimes do it on buses or planes. A handy option is to pop into a church, which can be an urban sanctuary regardless of beliefs. Often, if I'm preparing for a radio or TV appearance, I'll go into a bathroom cubicle and do a mini-meditation just to ground myself.

My favourite location is beneath a tree beside the stream in St Anne's Park in Dublin early on a sunny morning. I find the solitude of early morning and late night works best and I try to avoid eating, talking or checking the news before I start. Meditation is like 'logging on' to truth rather than logging on to my computer. I generally meditate sitting on a cushion with my back straight and legs crossed. Sometimes I do it standing up or sitting on a chair. I do a few basic stretches or yoga postures first so I'm alert.

Sometimes I light a candle and incense and put on a relaxation CD. I start with an intention for the meditation (for example, to be calm during a busy day), and then half close my eyes while looking down towards the candle or a random focal point. Occasionally I set a timer but mostly I don't. Some people use visualization techniques. I don't follow a set format or tradition. I make up my own rules but I've found great tips on courses and through books, DVDs and the internet.

No matter where or how you meditate, working with the breath is the key to success. The breath has the power to calm the body and slow the mind. I take gentle breaths from the lower belly up through the lungs. Now and then I'll repeat a mantra. It could be anything; for example, saying the words 'I am' when inhaling and the word 'connected' when exhaling.

Invariably, the monkey mind will jump in and try to ruin the party. It reminds me of the things I have to do that day, of the things I should have done the day before, and then takes me on some random adventure where I end up losing minutes thinking about buying a new jacket, or about someone who has annoyed me. Then I'll realize the monkey had me, and that's all right. The only way forward is to let go, let the thoughts flow by, and drop back into my meditation. Meditation is the art of calming traffic on a high-speed mental motorway. It takes time, patience, and practice.

During the day I sometimes get grumpy or irritated before realizing that I need to tune back in by focusing on my breathing. That's where the practice of mindfulness comes in. Mindfulness isn't quite focused meditation; it's rather the non-judgemental observation of thoughts, feelings, bodily sensations and whatever is happening around you. It is about awareness of the present moment, good or bad, and it can be practised when walking, working, eating, playing music or sports, and in everything you do. Ultimately mindfulness is about learning to live in the now, about 'being' rather than 'doing'. It is about being awake while accepting ourselves and each other.

Illness brought me to a turning point in my life. Meditation transformed me by helping me harness the incredible healing power of the mind. I believe the world is at a similar turning point. A silent and gentle revolution is needed, one that awakens us to truth and to the reality that the only time there is, is now. Meditation can create a new consciousness in business, politics, education and healthcare. Just as suffering and injustice originate in the mind, so too can peace. The magic of meditation can change minds and change the world.

1983 Dublin

Homeless dispossessed
women who have little rights
entitlement or power
challenging us
to listen
to change
to respond
to find our voice
Gifting us with their resilience
in the face of disaster
Their courage in the face of difficulties
pride in the face of poverty
dignity in the face of ignominy
self-respect in the face of rejection
hope in the face of little sign of change
Their prophetic cry for a life
where people reverence each other
where all live life to the full
where mercy and peace
and justice reign

All men are by nature equal, made all of the same earth by one Workman; and however we deceive ourselves, as dear unto God is the poor peasant as the mighty prince.

PLATO

The Samaritan Woman

At Jacob's well
a most unlikely ambassador
wrong time
place
race
religion
trusting the experience
believing the promise
courageously letting the old dreams die
becomes the prime witness
and proclaimer of the Good News
speaking from the edge
living the questions with faith and trust

Trust

Trusting the God
who watches and supports
the fragile caterpillar
becoming a butterfly

Road to Emmaus

Bewildered
unable to make sense of life
their whole world shattered
their dreams, hopes
promised future vanished
walking out of Jerusalem
to Emmaus
opening to a total stranger
Everything changed

Connectivity

Shaped from the same
goodness from which
the cosmos was created
A unique interdependence
God saw that it was good
challenging us
to recognize our place in the world

Oneness

Communion
union
oneness
you in me
me in you
completely one
living moving
and being
filled with the utter fullness of God

Present Moment

This one step
touching
embracing
cherishing the earth
walking into the now
this one
only
special
precious moment
with and through grace

Moment by Moment

Birthing the world each day
every second a new beginning
every moment a new creation
connecting and recreating
being transformed
through our every action
The creator
spirit
developing in us
a new consciousness
for this time

Morning

Waking early
rising with ease
breaking fast mindfully
in meditation and prayer
cradled in silence
held in stillness
strengthened for this new day

Emptying

Allowing God
to be God
my prayer
his prayer
transforming me
into her
fullness

Identity

Who from
Where to
seeking, searching, navigating and finding
. . . but not always
On the margins,
looking in
now on the periphery.
An unchanging horizon
in an everchanging world
The longing to belong
moment by moment

Síle Wall

Welcome

Being here
In this moment
this unexpected moment
Allowing life to happen
Now
Accepting what is
Giving it space
to find its home in me

Síle Wall

The Fragility of Life

In a lightning flash
the fragility of life bared
suddenly
in time's reality.

The devastation of typhoons and tsunamis
in faraway places.
Faces expressing shock
emotions numb
unprepared for doctors' diagnosis.
Swells of anger
guns fired, bodies maimed and lost.
Wars, suicide and oppression.
Refugee camps
full and overflowing
the pain of humanity embodied all around.
Talks and more talks
Fighting and more fighting
as the music of the heart
continues to perform in the background
symphonies of courage

Síle Wall

Courage

Touching the heart of fear
turning
negative energy
into creative action
scary doubts
into new initiatives
transforming wavering faith
into an unimagined future
a new rhythm emerging
ushering in the reign of love

*It had long since come to my attention
that people of accomplishment rarely sat
back and let things happen to them. They
went out and happened to things.*

LEONARDO DA VINCI

Contemplatives

Advocating for the world
a pebble
dropping
sinking
tapping
into the source
causing
ripples
of healing energy
over a
broken world

Waiting

God
cannot be
merited
God
available to all who
listen deeply
letting go
dying to all
waiting alone
feeling the hunger
in the dark empty spaces within
where he can be born

Love

When   your heart is broken open
        to the human
        in all its brokenness
        beauty
        and joy

When   you experience
        the pain of poverty
        and allow it to push
        your boundaries

When   you listen
        so deeply to the other
        that the distance between you
        (created by the mind) dissolves

When   you allow the
        brokenness of the other
        to touch your own brokenness

        then you will know love

Peace Making

A way of being
a vital human activity
promoting life
respecting the contrasts
of light and dark
shadow and glare
clamour and quiet
in every aspect of
creation

The Power of One

Reaching out
radiating joy
creating harmony
embodying hope
weaving a tapestry
of peace
and justice

Sitting

Resting in the harbour
quiet and still
one with its expanse
stretching outwards and onwards
Allowing planet Earth to become part of me
depth and height
darkness and light
waiting and accepting
as the breath of the universe
invites me into its rhythm
In and out
In and out

Síle Wall

Remaking the world

Seeking to
> understand
> strengthen
> comfort
> empathize
> increase trust
> listen deeply
> let go of vengeance
> rage against injustice
> stand with the weak
> offer forgiveness
> engender hope

Creating peace

Seeking Peace within not without

Peaceful thoughts
creating insight
Peaceful words
creating love
Peaceful actions
creating security
Being the peace we are
Being the peace
we want to see

Needs only one

A
single
seed
dying
bears
abundant
fruit

A single
heart
broken
heals
the
world

Health is the greatest gift,
contentment the greatest wealth,
faithfulness the best relationship.

BUDDHA

The Gift of Life

Síle Wall

At some time most of us question the meaning of life: where we are going, what we are part of, what life is all about. More often than not this questioning arises in the context of the traumas, both big and small, that life seems to throw our way. However, it can also arise in happy times – in times of celebration and times of togetherness. For me it usually comes as one of those fleeting, unexpected moments of insight, of mindfulness, that make themselves present when I am thoroughly absorbed in something else.

Recently I was in Dublin's Phoenix Park, walking without any particular direction, just attempting to be in the moment, when I was suddenly transported into pondering the meaning of life. Yes, I had been thinking a lot, but doing so mindfully. My walking, just for walking, became a new moment of consciousness.

It was early morning; visibility was reduced to a few feet on all sides as a dense fog encircled me. A mysterious presence in whispering sounds tried to engage with me. I seemed to be in the presence of what was known and unknown at the same time. Silent, graceful movements as the fog danced on the warming grass suggested the presence of beauty, the presence of wonder, the presence of awe, the presence of gentleness. At other times the movement of the fog appeared more aggressive and I experienced its coldness and density with unusual sharpness. I encountered flux and change; shadow and darkness; mystery and presence. I didn't rush. I took my time. I continued walking. I breathed in and breathed out. I was alive and grateful, in touch with the meaning of life, which my conscious self was not able to describe or my cognitive mind to define. I was reminded to 'remove the sandals from your [my] feet, for the place on which you [I] stood was holy ground' (Exodus 3: 5). Nature was my mentor opening me to the wonder of life and to the mystery of God in my life – a fleeting moment of awareness, of mindfulness, life a gift to be grateful for, a moment I allowed myself to feel.

We all know that life does not consist only of

experiences that make us resonate with joy, happiness and well-being. The reality of life for us and as it is lived by the other seven billion people around our world challenges any illusions we might have in that regard. Life has its ups but it also has its downs. It has its painful moments, and often pain-filled days. I have found that, with the practice of mindfulness, the mystery of life on both good and not-so-good days becomes an amazing gift. 'Be still and know.'

It is not easy to talk about life as a gift when life and death intermingle and merge in unexpected and heart-breaking ways. The path of human history embodies murder, rape, genocide, war, poverty, suicide, anguish, loss, dispossession and displacement, with thousands of people fleeing for refuge – perpetrators as well as victims. Human beings destroying life, creating atrocities in our time. The threads of life weave into one large tapestry of the human story as we listen to the radio, watch television or surf the net; and I am part of this story. I am part of its joy but I am also part of its suffering: 'we are all humankind, and our life is one,' Thich Nhat Hanh tells us. Each of us, in our own way, is living our 'one precious life' right here, now.

It is painful to see the suffering that flows throughout our world, hearts reaching out while minds try to understand. Thomas Merton in *Conjectures of a Guilty Bystander* teaches that 'the more I am able to affirm others to say "yes" to them in myself, by discovering them in myself and myself in them, the more real I am'. A moment of insight into the gift of life in the midst of our often broken world; a moment to learn 'I am', and that I am part of it.

I was drowned in an ocean of thought about life and its gift, and how best to write about it, when a friend, whom I would consider to be an expert in the field of life, rang the doorbell. Her visit came out of the blue. As we conversed, my busy mind slowed down and I grew attentive to her story with a new awareness and a quiet presence. We talked about many things, including the title of this essay. When she was a child, she told me, 'I don't ever remember feeling happy. There was so much upheaval and unhappiness in my life so I wouldn't look on it as a gift.'

She came from a family of thirteen children and following her father's death she and two of her siblings spent time in a convent in the Ireland of the 1950s. Her memory is that from then until the 1980s and even into the 1990s her life was in constant turmoil. In 1986 her fourth child was born. Throughout her first forty years she lived an insecure, unsettled life, all the while seeking a place to feel at home, within and without.

During our conversation she characterized herself as having no confidence, but, she said, 'I learned from my mum of a way to cope – this was alcohol and Valium. The drink gave me confidence but it also got hold of me.'

In 2000 she was diagnosed with multiple sclerosis and then in 2008 experienced severe burns when there was a fire in her apartment. Her life at that time hung by a thread but, as she said, 'I still soldier on. The fire was what I would call the gift of life.' Having given up the drink six years earlier she had recently been diagnosed with cancer, yet, she says, 'It doesn't faze me, my life is definitely a gift. I had to go through these things to appreciate life. I believe that we are all sisters and brothers and that we are sent into each other's lives to help each other. The past is gone, we have no future, we have today – maybe the full day – and the peace I feel when I realize this is a gift. I appreciate life, but not every day,' she tells me, giving life to words we tend to keep hidden in our heart.

The heart can incorporate the many dimensions of reality when we allow ourselves to accept what is unfolding within us and around us and to feel the pain that can be familiar and unfamiliar at the same time. A moment in time when the busy mind rests and learns to listen, receive and respond – receiving from and giving to the rhythm of life, its ups and downs, its twists and turns. When we are mindful we learn how to receive and how to reciprocate, how to accept and how to give thanks for what is now. To be truly alive . . .

As Marsha Edger says:

> You must still the mind's chatter,
> clear away the clutter, and
> live intuitively from the Soul.
> . . . To be truly alive means
> to fully engage in the moment.
> This moment,
> now, with an open heart
> filled with compassion and love.

The more real I am, the more alive I am, and the more my unique contribution brings to this world of ours, this world of joy and sorrow, of happiness and pain. How simple and yet how difficult. In this context living in the moment helps. When we are alert, aware, attentive and awake to our individual experiences of life, welcoming and accepting each one with compassion, loving-kindness and equanimity, then we are in tune with life and its gifts. Life puts in our path just what we need to know if we are mindful and understand how to receive what is unfolding within us and around us, as the story of my friend calling unexpectedly illustrates.

There are no easy answers to questions about the meaning of life. But through the practice of mindfulness we can explore and express our relationship with life. Life offers everything when we feel it, digest it and allow it to find a resting place within us. When we are mindful, even for one tiny minuscule of a second, we embody the immensity and wonder, the pain and heartache of the world we are part of, the miracle that is life. John O'Donohue once said, 'No day belongs to us. Each day is a gift.'

The following words of the American writer Wendell Berry nicely summarize my attempt to share some thoughts with you on life as a gift: 'I see that the life of this place is always emerging beyond expectation or prediction or typicality, that it is unique, given to the world minute by minute, only once, never to be repeated. And this is when I see that this life is a miracle, absolutely worth having, absolutely worth saving. We are alive within mystery, by miracle.'

Finding God in all Things

So immersed in thinking about God
we miss God
God steeped
in human experience
God continually revealed
through the silent unfolding story
of a changing
humanity
and universe

Spirituality is not to be learned by flight from the world, or by running away from things, or by turning solitary and going apart from the world. Rather, we must learn an inner solitude wherever or with whomsoever we may be. We must learn to penetrate things and find God there.

Meister Eckhart

Lonely

Isolated
    Distracted
    Disconnected
    Frightened
    Desolate moments
Alone
    Connected
    Rooted
    Focused
    Restored
    Wondrous Moment

Hope

seedbed
of resilience
releasing
energy
to
reshape
the
world

Swallow

Suddenly appearing
Frightened
Swiftly gliding
Hither and thither
Round and round
Seeking searching
Lost in a concrete box
Unfamiliar territory
Hard, cold
Resting in a crevice, not home
Flying here, there
Searching again
Seeking again
Resting again
Beginning again and again and again

Síle Wall

Legends

for Eavan Frances

Tryers of firesides,
twilights. There are no tears in these.

Instead, they begin the world again,
making the mountain ridges blue
and the rivers clear and the hero fearless –

and the outcome always undecided
so the next teller can say *begin* and
again and astonish children.

Our children are our legends.
You are mine. You have my name.
My hair was once like yours.

Eavan Boland

Presence

The presence
I bring to any moment
Gives it power to bless
to nourish
to change
an ordinary unnoticed moment
into a moment of beauty
feeding the soul

*The best thing about the future is that
it comes one day at a time.*

ABRAHAM LINCOLN

The Gift

One breath
a gift
not ours
bigger than us
one breath
breathing
in
with
and
through
the universe
freely given
freely giving
out of love
always present
empowering
creating
recreating
an endless stream
of new beginnings
calling to freedom
as befits a gift

Waiting

Waiting
Expectations on hold
– an unknown space

Feelings frayed and tense
– a known space

What can I do
Is there anything I can do?

What can be done
by whom?

The process of waiting
waiting in hope, desperation
expectation
and what else?

The process goes on and on
Some day, this waiting will be no more
as another waiting takes its place.

Waiting
Who are you?
Why do you carry so much soul pain?

Síle Wall

Eternal One

Ever with us
revealing the path of truth and love
opening our minds and hearts
to your way
as we strive
to ease
the burdens of our
brothers and sisters

Hope

Seeds of Hope
ray by ray by ray
given
shared
again and again
like the seed
broken
given
growing
each ray
extending
expanding
radiating joy
throughout the world

Meditation

Every meditation
moving us to a
simpler
deeper
more loving
integrated
authentic life
is holy and good
leading to
an inner experience
of the divine spirit
dwelling within

Soul

Boundless
without boundaries
not limited to time and space
everywhere at all times
hidden in
stars of sky
rays of sun
light of moon
movement of cloud
pulse of earth
warmth of animal
blade of grass
towering mountain
breeze and wind
all aspects of life
not bound by
mind or body
boundless

Community

Evolving experience
mindful of
who we are
whose we are
attentive listeners
compassionate presence
mutual fidelity
outward looking
supporting diversity
embracing a broken world
choosing life

Non-violence

Resisting oppression
not
   passive
   shaming
   blaming
   threatening
   projecting
   defeatist
accepting suffering
befriending brokenness
connecting with the fundamental oneness of all
creative
imaginative
hope filled
breathing peace

October 2013

'what is this amongst so many'
Cold
Hunger
weeping
aching
trembling
wet
malnourished
fragile
miserable
broken
powerless
struggling people
naming it as it is
situating us in truth

Standing with them
cowed by their suffering
heart aching with their pain
our voices silenced
powerless

(Continued)

sharing what we have
'what is this amongst so many'
Praying for a miracle

World Peace

Developing a new and compelling
alternative to the prevailing world view
Believing all things are possible
Choosing collaboration over isolation
common good over individualism
unity over division
hope over despair
In the reality of my daily life

What is morally wrong can never be advantageous, even when it enables you to make some gain that you believe to be to your advantage. The mere act of believing that some wrongful course of action constitutes an advantage is pernicious.

CICERO

Woman of Courage

Woman of courage
without a home
speak to me.

Speak to me
of aloneness
pain
the struggle to be.

Speak to me
about the weight of your bags
what you choose
and discard
hold
give away

in a language
I can know
and
reciprocate

Síle Wall

We have a choice

Belittling
undermining
dismissing
destroying
covering truth
exploiting
competing
destructing
fuelling hatred
releasing anger
nurturing fear
fostering suspicion
promoting division
creates violence

Understanding
strengthening
listening
supporting
standing with
cooperating

(Continued)

comforting
building trust
forming relationships
letting go of vengeance
offering forgiveness
creates peace

Openness

Opening to the presence of the Divine in all life
Loving all that life presents
Being fashioned in the image I love
embodying that image in the world
Bringing about the reign of love

A Home

That look on their faces
when finally they got the house
a place they can now call home
a place of their own
Two years in three separate hostels
Father mother and three children
and almost two years in one room in a B&B
nearly broke them
For such an outpouring of gratitude
I wish I had built, plastered
and painted it myself
That delight in their eyes
as they clutched the keys
each other and myself
urged me on to
commit again to
campaign more vigorously
serve more selflessly
die daily

In the Now of God

Attitude of mind
Orientation of heart
Transforming presence
Engendering new life
Transcending the world
Anchoring beyond
Not denying or accepting
Rather holding
Pain and darkness
Suffering and disaster
In the present moment
In the now of God
A dance between what is
and what could be
A dance with providence
The impossible becoming possible

Beauty

Deepest desire
of my human spirit
hidden
in the
reality of day to day ordinary life
Hidden in layers
of blindness
insensitivity
self centredness
greed
Hidden in
the threatened lives
of my suffering brothers and sisters

Peace

Peace comes from
being able to contribute
the best we have
the best we can
all that we are
Peace comes when
we give space
to empower the other to give
the best they have
the best they can
all they are
to create a better world
Peace comes from the
contribution of all
to all
peace
an inner experience
with infinite possibilities

Five enemies of peace inhabit with us –
avarice, ambition, envy, anger, and pride;
if these were to be banished, we should
infallibly enjoy perpetual peace.

PETRARCH

A Soul for Society

Sister Thérèse

*Your vision will become clear only when you
can look into your heart. Who looks outside, dreams,
who looks inside, awakes.*

CARL JUNG

The call of the contemplative is a call to come back to the heart, to live from within. If we are sick, we go to a doctor or a specialist, if we have a legal problem we consult a lawyer – we go to the expert in the field. When it comes to the subject of life, where can one go except to the source – God, the one who gave us life – and to his Son, Jesus, who came to show us how to live that life and live it to the full?

I will illustrate what I mean by 'living from within' through the simple Gospel story of Jesus meeting a

Samaritan woman at Jacob's Well. This story has profound messages about 'living water' – about Jesus revealing himself as the Messiah and inviting this woman to look into her heart.

Jesus and his disciples are travelling from Judaea to Galilee and on their journey they must pass through the hostile territory of Samara. It is hot, and Jesus is very tired. His disciples, big burly fishermen weathered by sun and storm, go on ahead into the town for food, leaving him to rest by Jacob's Well.

A Samaritan woman comes along. Although she is not called poor, she has had five husbands. To be rejected or forsaken even once, they say, is an incredibly painful experience. How then does this woman feel who has been used and rejected five times? How would any one of us feel? She is raw, she is wounded, she is fragile in her deepest centre, her heart – so what does she do? She erects a barrier around her pain and chooses to live 'outside herself' on the surface – her only safe place. But this leaves her wide open to her so-called lovers – her users. She is in their control.

Jesus engages her in conversation. He asks for water and when he speaks about 'living water' her response is swift – she wants to know how he can get this. He then asks her to fetch her husband. She must have felt a stab of pain, and embarrassment too – but the conversation continues and she tells Jesus how her people worshipped God on this mountain, then moves on to the Messiah and who he might be. We have to marvel at how this poor woman draws revelations from Jesus. We have to marvel too, at the way he empowers her to stay with him as he leads the conversation deeper and deeper – but she remains firmly entrenched on the surface. She handles this conversation well – who could guess what was happening inside her? – but something did, because when the disciples return with the food she slips away quietly and runs back to the town to tell everyone about her meeting.

And what did she tell them? About the living water? About his identity as Messiah? No! She says, 'Come and see someone who has told me everything I ever did.' Now, remember, the townspeople would have shunned this woman. She was, after all, regarded as a loose woman – yet now there is no shame or grovelling on her part. And why? Because for the first time in her life someone has seen her as she really is and still loves her. Don't we all know the ache to be seen as we really are and still be loved? She is wounded and sinful, but has not been judged or condemned. Far from it. Love and compassion from the heart of Jesus lead her into her own heart, her deepest centre, where she must be healed. And healed she was, and freed too. Her dignity restored, she can face those who have shunned her. She doesn't hug the experience to herself – she wants them to be gifted too. This caring comes from the heart of a woman who is in touch with herself and with the God who dwells within. Jesus has led her back into her own heart/soul as to an oasis. Her deepest centre, now a place of peace and refreshment, she yearns for others to experience the same gift. God, oneself, one's neighbour – she was reconnected – she belonged again.

Isn't this what we all need? To see ourselves as persons in search of community rather than cogs in the wheel.

Within each of us there is an oasis, a place of refreshment and peace – which brings me to the subject of contemplation. What is it? In a nutshell, it's about things we long for so much, search for too – but in the wrong place. It's about the deep and abiding joy and peace that come from being loved by God, and I stress that word 'experience'. It's not an intellectual knowing but an experience similar to that of two people who are in love. A single glance across a room can communicate that love. It's the difference between tasting a lovely glass of red wine and merely knowing all about it.

Some people are called to devote their entire lives to contemplation, responding to Christ's invitation to 'Come away by yourselves to a lonely place'. This is not a call to loneliness; it is a call to closeness – closeness to God, to oneself, to one's neighbour, to nature. How well Irish spirituality of old understood that! One only has to recall the greeting of the passer-by to the workers, 'God bless the work', or, on entering a house, 'God bless all here'. When one is in touch with one's self and with God, blessings flow from the heart – and where could they flow except to the neighbour?

As Dag Hammarskjöld once said, 'the longest journey on earth is the journey inwards'. Those who devote their lives to contemplation embark on this journey in a very real way. Outwardly, the contemplative life appears to be a life of utter simplicity. Six to seven hours each day are spent in prayer and outside of that time the members of a community engage in very simple, ordinary work into which prayer spills over, gradually transforming the whole day into one long prayer. What cannot be observed is the inner life, the journey within the heart. Leaving the world and entering a monastery is only the first step – leaving the 'world within' is the real challenge. We all have a world of hopes, dreams, desires, ambitions and jealousies within us and if we stop right here and observe a few moments of silence to get in touch with our inner selves, I wonder what we would find? Would there be more turmoil within than all the noise outside us?

On the inward journey all this has to be confronted, named and relinquished. We must be poor within so that we can create an inner space for God – to gain, as it were, power over his heart – and maybe that is why monasteries are often called 'powerhouses of prayer'. The relatively few people who embark on this way of life do not do so for themselves – their agonies, their ecstasies are for others. Their inner freedom and their deep love equip them to stand before God on behalf of the whole world, in praise, thanksgiving and intercession.

Contemplatives in the world
What then of the rest of us? The truth is, we all have a spiritual or contemplative dimension to our lives and it is precisely because this is so undernourished that everything else falls out of place, resulting in confusion and disillusionment, if not outright chaos.

We are highly aware of our physical life – endless glossy magazines tell us how to care for and pamper the body. But we have an emotional life and an intellectual life too. Holding all these lives together at their centre is the life of the Spirit – our 'contemplative dimension' – and this should be an oasis of peace and refreshment because, whether we believe it or not, God is there.

Our world is God's gift to us. Our country, our land with its people and its culture, is his gift to each one of us. The salvation of this human world lies in the human heart and in the integrity of the human soul. We need to care for life, to nurture it, develop it, beautify it – but how can we do this if we don't pause to see which way we are going, pause to think of the giver of the gift and what his intentions might be? And when we do pause, what do we see? We see that we are living in a world of rapid change.

We are told the generation gap is down now to just five years – the pace of life is swift!

We are living in a competitive society where the person who hesitates is definitely lost – the pace of life is risky!

We are living in a materialistic society where all that matters is that the goods are delivered no matter what the cost – the pace of life can be cruel!

Practical suggestions
How can I get off the treadmill? How can I get in touch with my deepest centre? There is no easy way. Choices

have to be made. Do I choose work, promotion, my salary increase, a bigger car – to the detriment of inner peace and quality time spent with my spouse and family? Can I take time to admire a sunset and say 'Thank you, God', or just be with a lonely or elderly person and let them know I care. Am I living from within, in control of my life, or am I on the surface, 'outside of myself', like the Samaritan woman, and in the control of the system?

One thing is certain: our lives can never have depth, quality, peace, or any measure of real success, unless we set aside at least fifteen to twenty minutes a day to get in touch with what is going on in our spirit – to get in touch with God. And as great as this need is to get in touch with our inner self, 'our contemplative dimension', is our need to have quality in-depth conversation with others, to nourish and encourage us on our journey. What we feed our minds on is what we pray about. What are we feeding our minds on? What is the quality of our reading and our viewing and how does it influence our lives, our prayer?

Simple suggestions, but putting them into practice requires great discipline. It is hard to be still, to go against the tide, but it is our sure road back to peace and serenity and our sure way of restoring the balance in society.

Vaclav Havel says we need 'to see the very earth we inhabit linked with heaven above us'. In conclusion, I leave you with this nugget of monastic wisdom:

Once upon a time, an ancient monastic tale says, the Elder said to the businessman, 'As the fish perishes on dry land, so you perish when you get entangled in the world. The fish must return to the water and you must return to the Spirit.' The businessman was aghast. 'Are you saying that I must give up my business and go into a monastery?' he asked. And the Elder said, 'Definitely not. I am telling you to hold on to your business and go into your heart.'

The Phoenix Park

Winter trees
fragile, transparent,
the ancient craft of lacemaking visible
in everchanging leaf patterns
under the blue grey sky
surrounding the polo grounds in Dublin's
Phoenix Park

Leaves motionless
veins twisted and looped
trees weaving pillars of brown, black and grey
nature punctuating winter
with moments of awareness

Síle Wall

Into Light

Embracing light and darkness
Knowing that in the darkest winter
summer is forming
Trusting the dark
I transform it
into light

Seeing with the Heart

Seeing with the heart
>The heart
>centre of all things
>centre of my being
>where I am
>at one with myself
>with others
>with the true spirit of love

Seeing with the heart
>always surprising
>no part too
>small
>simple
>ordinary
>everything becomes
>full of potential
>Full of possibility

Seeing with the heart
>experiencing the oneness of all

Listening to the voice within

The voice within speaks to us
where we are
giving clarity to the voices outside
inviting us to
  stop and listen to
  life's beauty
  fragility
  power
  the joys and sorrows of relationships
  suffering of our brothers and sisters
  exploitation of nature
  all around
The voice within helping us to respond
in the present moment
with integrity
courage
and fidelity

As we express our gratitude, we must never forget that the highest appreciation is not to utter words, but to live by them.

JOHN F. KENNEDY

Evening

Light of day getting darker and shorter
beginning to hear the heartbeat of winter
trees shedding their dying leaves
seeds resting in the silent earth
inviting me to ask
what needs to die in me
what in my life
do I need to let go
so that a new seed
can take root
grow
bud
blossom
seeding the future?

Balance

Perched on the edge of unknowing
risking moving out of
the familiar and secure
into a vast uncertainty
seeing myself
in a bigger context
I find a balance that
allows the unexpected to happen

Sanctuary

A quiet place in the heart
a place of peace
a place of stillness
a place to know who I am
At the core of my being
a place to be attentive
to the changes occurring inside me
to the changes occurring outside me
a place where past and future are
intertwined and transformed

Sacred Moments

Sacred moments
punctuating my day
saluting the stillness of
the tree outside my window
the birds picking the grain
on the other side of the window
feeling the breeze on my face
listening to the rustling leaves
stopping to look at the primrose
gazing at
the multicoloured dawning sky
frail fragile irises nodding on their stems
leaves falling dancing and scattering
without haste or form
these sacred moments
ground me
in the source of my being
connecting me
to the imperceptible movement of life

Voice of Truth

Pushing me to see differently
To hear in a different way
Challenging me to live with
    compassion
    love
    integrity
    and
    justice
reaching into the core of my being
compelling me to action

*There is one thing alone that stands
the brunt of life throughout its course:
a quiet conscience.*

EURIPIDES

Creation

an ongoing story
calling the world into being
a continuous process
a flash
a signal
every instant a new creation
my task to be attentive
to what is being born
to cooperate with
the birthing of a new earth
over and over giving birth to myself
God's dream in me for our world

Seeing with new eyes

Giving energy
and full attention
to each moment
concentrating on how we live each day
and who we are
knowing that what emerges
may not be what we envisioned
but what is right

Autumn

Reminding me that all things are transitory
everything moving and changing into the new
leaving beautiful spaces where something else lived
Trees letting go of their leaves
revealing an elegant emptiness
a naked beauty
Making visible the intricate precious detail
of abandoned birds' nests
Rays of sunlight transforming naked interlocking
branches
into exotic patterns
The wheel of life turning before my eyes
reminding me to surrender like the tree
to what will be
Grateful for what has been

Phoenix Park, early morning, December 2011

A light shines
on snowy beauty
A vast untouched carpet
of pristine white
Trees exhibit exquisite
white lanterns
reaching to the sky
grasped by what I cannot grasp
beckoning deep gratitude

'Rabbi I want to see'

To see all things
as part of the whole of life
To erase the duality that locks me
into seeing difference as division
To see the miracle of diversity
without judgement
To bring new sight to eyes blurred
by fear, prejudice and polarization
To open eyes wide
to the wonder of unity in diversity
Seeing all as one
in the oneness of our creator

The Seeker

Searching
Seeking
not unhappy yet not content
Exploring
hoping to find life's secret
Seeking peace in the stillness of mountains
seas, rivers and forests
Seeking to live in relationships
where love can be embraced
love that will not impede my searching
prevent my seeking
lock my imagination
that will take me for who I am
Searching for the ultimate

Gentling

Today I will walk gently on the earth
Opening my vision
To see beyond the surface
to the sacredness of life
Gentling my listening
To hear what lies beneath
and beyond the world
Gentling my touch
to feel the fears and joys of life
Gentling my taste
to know what is bitter and sweet
Gentling my thinking
that I may be present in the moment
Gentling my voice
that the frightened may hear
Gentling my steps
that I may walk mindfully
Gentling my welcome
that the vulnerable may enter
Gentling my movements
making space for the other
Gentling my heart
that I may be open to all

Exclusion

Queuing –
Rain beating down on brokenness
In all its fragility
Faces uncommunicating
Young boys and girls
Men and women
Waiting –

Waiting –
Steaming, drying
Material needs being met
By papers, questions
Here, not there
A fag, a light
At your discretion
Not my right

Feeling –
Awkward and uneasy
Out-of-home
Eyes frightened
Furtively seeking
a language communicating
Love   *Síle Wall*

Loneliness

Loneliness of Soul
loneliness of mystery
reaching to the infinite
with finite words
Loneliness of being loved
by whom we cannot see or comprehend
Loneliness of facing alone
the darkness of one's own humanity
Loneliness that cannot ever be understood
or defined
Loneliness of longing for a place
of unending love and peace
a yearning
for something beyond

Homelessness

No place of my own
no bed
no chair
walking in the waste
or wind and rain
grabbing the crumbs
where someone else has eaten
clutching the coins
for food and shelter
sharing the little I have
waiting for someone
to acknowledge my existence
look me in the eye
call me by name
yearning to belong
to feel connected
needed
respected
yearning to be more than
a bed

a number
a meal
yearning for somebody to care

care that I am hungry
care that I am thirsty
care that I am cold
care that I am wet
care that I am sick
care if I die tonight

Refugees

Forty-five million refugees displaced
dispossessed
Poor suffering humanity
Exiled from the world
Exiled from their homeland
family and friends
Exiled from their bodies
raped and abused
Exiled from themselves
Anguished and emotionally
unable to understand or accept
who they are
Exiled from each other
Saying goodbye
not knowing if they will ever meet again
Holding a vision of home in their hearts
braving unspeakable cold, hunger, thirst, want
in the hope of reaching a new home

Let the morning bring me word of your unfailing love, for I have put my trust in you. Show me the way I should go, for to you I lift up my soul.

PSALM 143:8

Moments of Grace

The silence of God
joy of birth
desolation of death
joy of forgiveness
darkness of life
tenderness of love
loneliness of pain
comfort of friendship
disappointment of infidelity
generosity of spirit
ingratitude of others
all human experiences
moments of grace
opening me to
the transcendent
God
the mystery
in all human experience
when I am most human
I experience God

Nature's Gift

Mindful of nature
Alive to the mystery of change.
Each day offering innumerable opportunities

Rain falling
Sensation of wetness
Gentleness of touch
Sun rising
Sensation of warmth
Beauty of vision
Flower opening
Sensation of presence
Fragrance of smell
Bird singing
Sensation of tone
Nourishment of sound
Berries ripening
Sensation of tingling
Effortless desire

Síle Wall

Living a life which includes death

Challenging me to accept my mortality
to appreciate and reverence
everyone and everything
To celebrate life's moments
as they come
knowing that each
is part of the eternal moment
Seeing all of life in perspective
facing the ultimate questions of life
Who am I?
Who have I become?
Who do I want to be?
What is significant now?
Causing me to go deeper
to move beyond the surface of things
touching into my soul
connecting me to the core of my being
calling me to
confront my fears and anxieties
befriend the reality of the unknown
let go of all that is not essential

to receive each day
as a new opportunity
for my love to grow deeper
and less conditional

Faithful Love

Challenging my own commitment
inspiring myself to greater fidelity
reflecting the infinite fidelity of God
always
accepting
gracious
understanding
kind
never
    lying
    deceiving
    betraying
    or abandoning
as the dawn
    shining light on everything
    enfolds and opens
    my heart to wonder

Born again

Suddenly
utterly
vulnerable
alone
separated
cold
hungry
lost
terrified
in the face of an unknown world
each letting go
of the safe secure certain familiar
invites me to be born again
each change summoning me
to an inner transformation
the more radical the change
the more potential
for discovering another aspect
of my inner selves

a continuous process of birthing

Gratitude

For all these I say thank you
    eyes that see and gaze
    ears that delight in voice and sound
    taste buds enjoying the pleasures
    of eating and drinking
    nose which receives each breath of life
    hands that love to feel and touch
    Friends who
    accept and love me as I am
    support and encourage
    me on this great journey of life
    The generosity of others
    whose words and actions
    come at the right time
    The privilege of being able to use
    my gifts for the service of others
    The basic necessities of life
    The miracle of night and day
    light and darkness
    For knowing that I can influence
    the fate of the world
    and create peace on earth
    by my daily choices and actions

Soul

The quest for immortality
In the face of mortality
The quest for beauty
In the face of darkness
The quest for truth
In the face of superficiality
The quest for depth
In the face of shallowness
The quest for hope
In the face of despair
The quest for light
In the face of darkness
The quest for peace
In the face of violence
The quest for the spiritual
In the face of the all too material
The quest for silence
In the face of noise
The quest for stillness
In the face of chaos
The quest for being
In the face of doing

Prayer

A matter of the heart
not the head
Loving more
thinking less
surrendering more
asking less
listening more
speaking less
recollected more
distracted less
Touching into the deep strong
peaceful well within

Body of Christ

Body of Christ
God
incarnate in creation
this new body
filled with the fullness of Christ
fullness overflows into fullness
body into body
I into we
love into love
When one part suffers
all parts suffer
When one part loves
all parts love
All dualism gives way
to the interrelatedness of God
and all creation
Christ not just an object of worship
but the energy amongst us
All creation
healed and graced
to form one body

The ground we walk on, the plants and creatures, the clouds above constantly dissolving into new formations – each gift of nature possessing its own radiant energy, bound together by cosmic harmony.

RUTH BERNHARD

Meditation

Korko Moses, SJ

Sit quietly in a relaxed way,
look in front of you at the vast expanse of green,
hills or the sky . . .
look at the colours, shades of colours . . .
listen to the sounds that come from far and near . . .
listen also to the silence on which the sound comes floating;
do not think about them,
just be present to them . . .
become aware of the breeze that touches your skin . . .
become aware of your breathing . . .
take a deep breath and breathe out slowly,
do this for a few times;
be with your normal breath for a few minutes
without any thinking . . .

In these few minutes you will have forgotten your problems, worries and the concerns of your life; you will have felt a sense of peace and well-being. From where did this peace come? From nowhere; it is already in you. This brief awareness practice has cut off all your wandering thoughts, enabling you to get in touch with your deeper, real self of peace, serenity and joy. Already in this exercise you have got a taste of meditation.

Life today has become a complex one of increased communications, competition and individualism; full of worries, speed, noise and endless activities that create tension and aggression. Here meditation is useful. Meditation takes us to a world free of all care and concern, where there is no ambition, and no struggle. Today people all over the world are drawn to meditation. Overcoming cultural and religious barriers they want to make direct contact with the truth of their real self.

Ignorance of our real nature is at the root of all suffering and is maintained by our mind's habitual tendency to wander. By making the mind one-pointed, meditation awakens us to our true self. The journey from our narrow, normal consciousness to a broader, higher consciousness of our true self merging with the Cosmic Self is meditation.

We reach this state in various ways – perhaps by

reciting a mantra or the name of God, or by breath awareness, breath regulation, or fixing the mind on divine qualities such as love, compassion and omniscience. There are numerous forms of meditation – yogic, Buddhist Vipassana or Zen, tantric, Christian or Sufi meditation and Ignatian contemplation, among others. Any of these, when practised with detachment – that is without egoistic desires – can lead us to a space deep within us.

Any method can be learned under the guidance of someone who has reached the higher consciousness through meditation practice. There are various starting points; for example, doing one's duties mindfully without self-centred interest for the welfare of the world and the Glory of God (karma yoga); surrendering oneself to God and trying to do his will (bhakti yoga), or seriously reflecting on the question 'Who am I?' (jnana yoga). Each will eventually lead to inner silence and then to the higher consciousness known as self-realization, God experience, enlightenment or *satori samadhi*.

The Upanishads speak of four levels of consciousness – from the first level where one is aware of the joy and satisfaction experienced when the senses come into contact with the external world; through joy that comes through the mental world of memories, fantasies, and so on; to the third level, of joy that arises solely from within, with no connection to the body or the mind, like great joy after a deep, dreamless sleep. On the fourth level one experiences the cosmic oneness which there are no words or language to describe. The journey from the first level to the fourth level of consciousness is the process; and the purpose and goal of meditation.

At the third level of consciousness all sorrow and suffering come to an end. One experiences the harmony of body, mind and spirit within, and harmony with the world outside. One sees goodness in all people and events, God in all beings and all beings in God, and comes forward to serve the Lord in serving people; the unity behind apparent diversity can be seen. This holistic vision of reality can energize a person to such an extent that they can do extraordinary things – knowing the past and future, healing others and living a physically and mentally healthy life. Of course, such external benefits attract people who hope to gain higher powers for their own benefit – to have a tension-free physically healthy life, achieve fame, succeed in business or accumulate more wealth. Sad to say, these people have not understood the real purpose of meditation. Perishable material benefits are worthless in comparison to the bliss of superconsciousness. It is important that those who learn meditation keep the supreme goal clear in their mind. Meditation is not for personal benefit: the enlightenment it brings is for the welfare of the world; that is why we end all meditations with the words '*May all beings be happy, may all people live in peace and in harmony*'.

Often meditation is understood as reflection on a passage from Scripture or as a way to reform one's life. But the meditation we are talking about here is a journey towards silence. Meditation, or Dhyāna, here is defined as the maintenance of an unbroken current of thought on a definite object or theme to the exclusion of other thoughts. The word combines *dhi* (the intuitive faculty) + *yan* (journey) to mean the journey of the intuitive mind. The word 'meditation' comes from the Latin root *meditare*, 'to go to the centre'.

Many people start meditation practice enthusiastically but give up after a while or go astray, or they may even harm themselves. Silent meditation or contemplation has to be learned personally from someone who is advanced in meditation, a guru, and must be practised under guidance for a long time. Before starting one has to live a life based on sound moral principles, doing one's duty faithfully at home and in society. For progress in spiritual life according to the

Yoga Sutras of Patanjali, certain detailed rules also have to be observed, from non-violence to cleanliness and austerity. It's also important that the body is healthy and that you are relaxed enough to be able to sit still for a long time. The exercises designed for this (*asanas*) are popularly known as yoga.

Correct breathing is very important as the vital force of the universe (*prana*) has to be regulated through breath control. This has many beneficial effects – including reducing stress and soothing the central nervous system. Because breath and mind are connected, when the breath is regulated mind control becomes easy. Various methods of meditation such as breath awareness or mantra repetition train the mind until it can remain still for short periods of time. With more practice, the period of silence increases. When silence can be maintained for hours then one experiences *samadhi* – total union.

'The essential is hidden from the eyes.' The rational mind, with the help of our five senses, can see only passing reality, which is constantly changing. It can't perceive what is permanent because the mind itself is a product of impermanence. The faculty of intuition – called *buddhi* in the East – is capable of perceiving the permanent, once the rational mind is silenced. However, to silence the mind requires a lot of practice, as well as complete self-mastery and a great longing to know the Ultimate Truth. Meditation is the road to enlightenment. Through meditation we can see permanence in impermanence, silence in sound, and change in stillness.

Impermanence comes from permanence and goes back to the permanent, which is God. That which comes from God is also God. So the permanence as well as the impermanence are one and the same God. The Upanishad says,

Poornam adah poornam idam poornat poornam
udachate,
Poornasya poornamadaya, poornameva avashisyate.

Fullness here, fullness there, from fullness comes fullness. Removing fullness from fullness, fullness alone remains.

May all beings be happy

Be happy for this moment.
This moment is your life.

OMAR KHAYYAM

Global Village

Photographs
taken by astronauts
millions of miles away
revealing the
oneness
unity
harmony
balance
of this sacred planet
our global village
not out there
but in us
as we are in it
mandala
our global village
our common soul
needing protection

Transformation

Open
so that the mystery
enters and penetrates me
Empty
so that my heart becomes softer
my desires deeper
my whole being
craving the mystery
depth is possible
transformation happens

Sanctuary

Deep within me
is an amazing
inner sanctuary
to be discovered
to be awakened
a holy place
a divine centre
to which I may
continually return
uniting me
with all humanity
with all creation
calling me to listen
to pay attention to
the eternal in our heart
reminding me
of my destiny
calling me home

A Bountiful God

The infinite Bounty of God

gifting us with life

not merited

for the benefit of all

to bring about

the transformation

of the world

a world of

peace

justice

and love

Trust

Being vulnerable
not trusting
afraid of being
betrayed
abandoned
crushed

Being vulnerable
trusting
bringing me closer to others
opening me to new possibilities

Before betrayals
and disappointments
I trusted another
with the very substance
of my life

Mystery

Wholeness of life
Enmeshed

Interwoven
Constantly striving
Moving out, moving on.
New in the unfamiliar
Deeper, changed.
New in newness
Within and beyond
Mysterying itself

Síle Wall

Seeing

It's not what you look at that matters, it's what you see.
Henry David Thoreau

Seeing with attention
is to see the
real
unique
the important
seeing with attention
always creative
always transforming
never neutral
giving energy
giving life
colouring perception
colouring life

Life

I am part of it
and it is part of me
I am part of the moving rivers
the roaring seas
and they are part of me
I am one with the highest reaches
of the sky
one with the formation of rain
and it is part of me
one with every breath I breathe
I am at one with all of life
this air I breathe in is you
this air I breathe out is me
this air we share
I give life to you
and you give life to me
all life passes through me
and I through it
every human person
every living being
every creature

(Continued)

163

insect
plant
is part of me

and I am part of them
no part is separate
I am part of the devastated rainforests
the endangered species
I am one with Aida
the hungry child in Homs
I am one with Marie
who lost everything in Tacloban
Eternal word
Eternal heart
Eternal one
I reach out and touch you
in all the creatures
and creations
that have come to life
through you
each of us living within you

Generosity is giving more than you can,
and pride is taking less than you need.

KAHLIL GIBRAN

Holy One

You are my delight
my hope
You are the light
of my soul
the joy in my heart
the dwelling place
of all that is good
you are the beginning
and end
the source of light
the fountain of life
the indestructible energy
that fuels the cosmos

You are the giver of life
Fountain of light
Source of all courage, strength and peace
Heart of the universe
Boundless in blessing
Total in giving
Unconditional in loving

Endless in forgiving
Infinite in compassion
Enduring in mercy
Eternal cause of all things
Lover of all
Open my heart
To let go of fear
To let go of control
To surrender
To trust
To receive all that is offered

God's Dream

In the innermost core of my being
I have an inner dream
God dreaming in me
From all time
For all time
For this our world
To know this dream
I am called to listen deeply
To listen honestly
To the still small voice within
Guiding me to dream this dream
To be this dream
To be a co-creator
In the world

This Moment

What I do now
will affect my whole life
today
tomorrow
in years to come
everything that is
is contained in this moment
past
present
promise
future
everything that is
to be had in life
is already here
Learning to
be in this moment
determines
the quality of my life now
and in the future
it is being fully awake
using this time

(Continued)

this moment
in ways that deepen
rather than fragment me

It is being concerned now
with the fundamental things
that last
It is making room in the present
for the things that are eternal
It is recognizing what is valuable
for the life of the soul
It is doing what I need to do now
not everything I can do

Disappointments

Trauma tragedies and disappointments
shake my certainties in life
Each of them shape me
They can make me open to a new reality
or close my mind and heart
They can toughen
season
temper
harden
or soften me
I always have choice

Life

Life is simply about life
It is the creator in creation
God's life incarnate in the world around us
the holiness of everyone
and everything
reflecting the nature of God
every step a coming home

The Storm

Lightning flashing
thunder pealing
winds crashing
rain pouring
seas roaring
trees and plants bowing
and bending to the ground
animals seeking safety
dogs barking
birds hiding
children crying

Silence

To be silent and utterly alone with myself
can be frightening
until I realize that silence draws me gently into
the very depth of myself

Until I know that letting go of words
draws me into the one word made flesh

To be silent alone
is to discover a new depth within
To be silent with others
is to go into a greater depth together

Mountain Mist

Creating mystery
Swirling downwards
Dancing
Skating
Enveloping
Embracing
Protecting
Shielding
then – slipping away

Revealing the beauty of humanity
Within a transformed mountain top

Síle Wall

Prayer

When I pray
I surrender
I am silent
I listen
I am at home with myself
Returning again and again
to the breath
to emptiness
to fullness
Being held and embraced
By the sacred

*Sit quietly, do nothing, spring comes
and the grass grows by itself.*

ZEN SAYING

Criticism

Always looks me in the eye
Always an opportunity to learn
Only I can choose
to react with self pity
or to look for the deep truth
Only I can choose
to let the criticism harden my heart
or set me free
Only I can choose to look at myself
with humble open loving reflective eyes
Open to the new
Open to change

Hope

radiating
flowing
lifting
what is dead in me

Hope
breathing
through me
filling my lungs
carrying me
as I wait and wait
for a new rhythm
a new light
a new dawn

No Unimportant Moment

There is no unimportant moment
nothing
no thing
person
expression
thought
joy or pain
That cannot be harvested
for nourishment
for myself and others
On this journey
every moment is
a sacred step
to wholeness
May I experience
every moment fully
letting it energize me
as I energize it
letting it bless me
as I bless it

This Day

The womb of the morning
Dawn breaking
a glimmer across the sky
a glow
unfolding in its own time
the light of the world
slowing me down
reminding me
of the little spark
waiting within
to be kindled

May I kindle this inner spark today
light this light
may it shine
like the sun rising in the east
planting seeds of love
enlightening my mind to see
illuminating my heart to love
saying yes to the unfolding work
of our creator God

True friendship

To reach out in love
with the power
desire
will
impetus
the determination
to forget myself
for another's sake
to hold another
in greater esteem than myself
Feeling the
fear
pain
suffering
of and with the other
risking my life for another
True friendship depends on this

Thousands of candles can be lighted from a single candle, and the life of the candle will not be shortened. Happiness never decreases by being shared.

BUDDHA

Compassion to Self

As I strive to
become more fully human
may I accept my less than perfect self
may I accept my weaknesses
as my greatest treasure
keeping me humble
detaching me from my ego
May I look to myself this day with kindness
be loving and gentle
With my
clumsiness
slowness to change
hardness of heart
anxiety
resentment
harsh judgement
self pity
negativity
and with anything that keeps me
from receiving joy this day
may I become compassionate towards myself
as I slowly grow to wholeness

Divine Life

Life surging through
the vine and its branches
through my whole being
God out there
living moving and being in all

Gratitude

Gratitude helps me to
keep perspective
to make connections

Gratitude comes from the heart
where I am rooted in universal belonging
engaging my whole person
Taking nothing for granted
Gratitude is life

Kate

Mine
A washed wool shawl
Cerulean, cobalt, cornflower, skyblue
mixed with lime green
a present
my friend cares.
Half a century
before now
taken from family
a child of four
continues to live with
the pain of rejection
broken ties
damaged body
enquiring mind
mine, my shawl, my friend.

Síle Wall

The Way of the Spirit

The way of the Spirit
is
the
way of emptiness
Emptying the
inner debris
negativity
doubts
endless clutter
crowding my inner space
blocking my inner growth
The way of the Spirit
is
the
way of emptiness
opening to the vast immense
mysterious depth within me
filling me with awe
beauty
wonder
surprise
helping me transcend the barriers

separating me from others
from God
stretching me
to the infinite

Forgiveness

To forgive is letting go
A growing awareness
that I am not in control of other people
Forgiveness
beyond the human
a gift
a grace
a blessing greater than myself
to seek and pray for

Stillness

In each of us there is a centre of stillness
Enfolded in Silence
Silence and stillness
like many of life's most important elements
Air, sea, flowers, mountains,
cannot be valued in material terms
In this quiet core where God's spirit dwells in us
God lives, moves and has being
In this innermost centre of our being
We are most deeply and
profoundly known and loved by God
It is where God attaches to us
And we attach ourselves to God

Stillness growing and deepening with awareness
Leading us to a calm serenity
Moving us into life in a new way
to where the turbulent waters of life are quietened

The door to inner stillness is everywhere
is here

Seeing with the Heart

Seeing with the Heart
All of life is surprise
nothing too small
simple
mundane
ecstatic
exalted
ordinary
or extraordinary
All is surprise

Seeing with the heart
we see with an inner eye
accepting and greeting
each person and event
with surprise
with full awareness

Hope

Hope is believing beyond today
encouraging me to follow my dreams
trusting that what is happening
will eventually make sense
nudging me when it is time to move on
encouraging me not to give in
finding the truth about myself
in the midst of darkness
accepting my own mortality
Hope accepts mystery
Hope offers solid trust in the unknown

My Father, the Farmer, the Sower

The sower is a person of hope
loves the seeds into life
waiting for life to emerge
releasing life
saying yes yes yes
to every plant being born

The sower is a person of hope
waiting with conviction and expectations
not concerned with success
living on the edge
sowing seeds
The sower may fail and fail and fail again
but will try and try again
and in the trying
the sower is a light to the world

*The will to win, the desire to succeed,
the urge to reach your full potential . . .
these are the keys that will unlock the
door to personal excellence.*

CONFUCIUS

Why We Need a Spirituality

Peter McVerry

I understand spirituality to be an expression of the way in which we relate to others, to our world and, ultimately, to God. Everyone has a spirituality, even if it is not articulated. Many who do not believe in God live very happy, fulfilled lives, giving of themselves to their family, to the community and to the world around them. They may have a rich spirituality, but one that excludes any relationship with a being we call God.

A young homeless man once said to me: 'The very thought that there might be a God depresses me.' Now, young people regularly tell me that they don't believe in God, but this was going a step further. Eventually, I came to realize what this man was trying to say – he felt so bad about himself that he was unlovable. How did he come to believe that? Well, it was the message he was getting from everyone around him: his family showed him no love, his school expelled him, the police kept moving him on. So he said to himself: 'If there is a God, God is looking down on me and saying, "there's someone I couldn't love"', because that is what he believed was the truth. And so he went on: 'It's bad enough going through life believing you are unlovable, but to have to go through eternity believing you are unlovable, that's too much.' The good news for him would be that there is no God, no afterlife; when you die, that's it, all the pain is over.

That young man's spirituality could not possibly include belief in God, yet he still has a vibrant spirituality.

Many people have a false understanding of God. They see God as a Being who has laid down laws that he expects us to obey and who promises us that, if we obey them, we will be rewarded with a place in heaven, but if we disobey them God's anger might consign us to a place called Hell. Their relationship with God is based on the fear of his disapproval or even anger. A life-giving spirituality cannot include a relationship with such a God.

I can only try to articulate my own need for a

spirituality which includes a belief in God and a relationship with God. Ultimately, the question I keep asking myself – and, I think, one that we all ask ourselves – is 'Why am I here? What is the purpose of my life?'

Either the meaning of life is given to us from outside ourselves, through the belief in a God or a higher power, or we invent that meaning. Either way, we can live very happy and fulfilled lives. However, if we deny the existence of a Being outside ourselves, a Being many of us call God, who gives meaning to our lives, then to find meaning in living for others is an arbitrary choice, even if it is a noble one. Others may find meaning in life by making as much money as possible, or having as much enjoyment in life as possible, seeing other people and our world as of value only in so far as they promote these objectives. All these choices, being arbitrary, are of equal validity, because there are no objective criteria to decide between the different meanings that people may give to life.

For me, God is a being who loves me with an infinite, unconditional and unchanging love. My belief in such a God comes from reflecting on my life, a life that has been filled with gifts. My belief in such a God fills me with a deep peace that nothing, and no one, can disturb. Even if there were no God, believing in God would achieve one of my deepest desires in life, namely to find peace!

That is the good news. The bad news is that everyone else is loved by God with the same infinite, unconditional and unchanging love – even people I don't like or want anything to do with. So this defines my relationship with others. Everyone, not just my family and friends, deserves to be treated with respect and dignity. Everything we have is a gift. None of us chooses where or when our existence begins or ends, or what gifts or talents we will have while here on earth. In my spirituality, we are given those gifts and talents, not so that we can use them just to have a good time but so that we can use them for the benefit of others, as well as ourselves. To want to love and care for others, to reach out to those who are rejected and unwanted in society is a consequence of my belief in God.

The meaning of life, for me, is to make our world a better place, to reduce the suffering that so many have to experience, to bring joy to others, especially those who need it most. This involves a commitment to working for justice. All injustice is a denial of the dignity of the person; poverty, homelessness, marginalization, discrimination and oppression are consequences of distorted relationships with other human beings, whom we see as of less value and less importance than ourselves.

This world is a gift from God. We have a responsibility to future generations not to make it uninhabitable. One of the greatest heartaches in working with homeless people is to see a person throw away the opportunity that a new home offers to them and return to homelessness. A few lose interest in maintaining their home and let it go to rack and ruin; a few others smash up and damage the very structure which is necessary to support them. The failure to respect that which is essential to the quality of their life and their future leads them back to nothingness.

So too, with our planet. Our failure to respect the home we have been given is putting all our futures at risk. Consumption was a disease people died of in the nineteenth century, but consumption of a different kind became a way of life in the twentieth and twenty-first centuries. We have impoverished our planet and ourselves – we have bigger houses and more broken homes, higher incomes and lower morale, more health resources and less well-being. Affluence, just as much as poverty, is a disease that is killing us and our planet.

To destroy the planet is to throw this gift back in

God's face as if it were of no worth. Destruction of the planet is a form of blasphemy.

And so an authentic relationship with others compels us to work for justice, to bring new life and new hope to those who are poor or marginalized in our world, and to ensure the possibility of life for those not yet born.

Compassionate listening is to help the other side suffer less. If we realize that other people are the same people as we are, we are no longer angry at them.

THICH NHAT HANH

Listening to the Earth

The Earth speaks only to those who
listen with their hearts
The Earth speaks in
a thousand ways
messages without words
the language of love
in the shape of a new leaf
the feel of a stone
the colour of the evening sky
the smell of summer rain
the sound of the night wind
the Earth speaks to everyone yet
only those who listen deeply
can hear and respond
The Earth speaks in surprise
The surprise of rainbows and waterfalls
of moon and sunrise
of air and water
of snowflakes and icicles
and in the constantly rich
unfolding and refolding of cloud

The voice within

Time spent in solitude is time
to listen deeply
to listen without
doing
without
being busy
planning and analysing
theorizing and judging
To listen deeply
is to be open to the moment
to hear the still small voice within
The voice of the intuitive heart

To listen deeply
is to tune into the cries of my heart
staying with those cries
learning how to respond
To listen deeply
is to become aware of the greater consciousness
the greater wisdom of which I am part
and which is part of me
becoming aware

(Continued)

201

of the interconnectedness
of all creation
the creator at work within all

To listen deeply
is to hear the call to move
beyond the limits of my humanity
grasping tiny fractions
of my ultimate identity
as child of God

To listen deeply
is to hear the call
to be the unique lovable person
I am called to be
to be free
to be real
to enter the liberty of the spirit

Finding Ourselves in Solitude

Silence and Solitude is a time
for intimacy with myself
to befriend myself
to embrace myself
bring me home to myself

In Silence and Solitude I come
face to face with myself
my soul laid bare
facing my inner compulsions
manipulative ways
mixed motivations
I see what I could be
but am not
what I want to be
and have failed to become

In Silence and Solitude
I come to a new depth
a new self awareness
accepting myself as I am

(Continued)

facing my own fear

my inner poverty and brokenness

my strengths

my energy

my spirit

embracing who it is I am

In Silence and Solitude

I find deep down inside myself

a microcosm of all the hopes and fears

joys and sorrows

pain and delight

of the whole universe

In Silence and Solitude

I can listen beyond the chaos

inside and around me

Tuning in

I make space

for deep knowing

touching into

the eternal harmony of the universe

existing beneath the chaos

of my everyday life

Unseen

Unnoticed
a seed stirs
life moves
sending its roots
into an unknown abyss
deep within . . .
An inner experience
Consciousness evolving

Síle Wall

Love

Only love can bring me to
perfect completion
Only love can bring me to
complete possession of myself
Only love can
unite me with what is deepest in me
Only love can
stretch me to embrace the totality of everyone
and everything on earth

Peace

Peace is here
in this moment
Now
Peace is what is
without judgement

Peace not in some other place
some other time
some other heart
Not to be sought after
not to be attained
Peace is already here in this moment
where everything that is
is accepted and welcomed

The World's Suffering

To wake up
to the world's suffering
I must listen
to hear
in the innermost part
of my being
The cry of
hunger
thirst
cold
wet
poverty
powerlessness
dispossession
struggle
desperation
injustice
hurt
pain
fear
anger

(Continued)

loss
shame
grief

wounded dignity
wounded pride
wounded respect
I must listen to the cry
of being ignored
of being put down
of being insulted
of being scorned
I must listen to the cry
of uncertainty
of anguish
The cry of the heart

look
listen
and you will hear
the voice of suffering
everywhere

Start by doing what's necessary; then do what's possible; and suddenly you are doing the impossible.

FRANCIS OF ASSISI

Kindness

Kindness
a natural resource
an energy on par with
water
wind
oil
solar
nuclear
energy

a treasure to be cherished
to evoke
to harness
to teach
to publicize
to turn into a fashion

Generosity

To be generous is risky
crossing a line of no return
Generous giving
is an irreversible act
of saying yes
There is no turning back
We give ourselves
Giving that is
conditional
cold
or half-hearted
is a contradiction
In the moment
of generous giving
nothing is spared
we give all

Joan

Life
Tragedy stalked you
within and without
after and before.
Humanity stirring
groaning
hitting back, hitting out
Battling to ensure
birth and death
meet
embrace
disentangle
confront
Each in its own space.
finding rest
after hours
Days
Months
Years
of surviving.
Wit, laughter, humour
Humanity at play

Síle Wall

Emptiness

I come before you seeking peace
I ask to be filled with
your presence
your love
your peace
I come to be filled
I wait in silence
I listen
Slowly my life is laid bare
before me
Slowly I discover
I have no more space
I am already too full
I am full of things
that keep you out
I am full of
opinions and attitudes
of fears
resentments
and
control
I am full of self pity
and arrogance

(Continued)

213

I am full of myself
with no room for you
I hear I have to let go
let go
let go
of all that hinders
my wholeness
of all that hinders
your life in me
You help me slowly
to identify and overcome
one by one
the barriers
the obstacles
the hindrances
to your life in me
You help me
to empty myself
of myself
to make space
for my true self
to make space
for peace and joy and love
to make space
for you

Wisdom

Beneath the surface of my life
there flows a stream of inner wisdom
It flows like an underground river
from one end of my life to the other
Gained through the experiences of people
and events in my life
dormant until brought to consciousness
It is unique and personal
accessible only to me
available only through the silent voice
speaking in my heart
through this inner wisdom
I discover what is true
and worthwhile in my life

Of all human activities, man's listening to God is the supreme act of his reasoning and will.

POPE PAUL VI

True Relationships

True relationships
    influenced by the way
    I see and feel about myself
    determined by who I believe I am
True relationships
    reflecting back to others
    a sense of their own beauty
    inviting them to believe in themselves
True relationships
    bringing
    peace
    beauty
    order
    and
    balm

Stranger

Sleeping outside
in the crevice
of a church building
along a busy street.
Today hobbling towards
your first meal of the day
in one of Dublin's eating houses.
Feet bandaged
In shoes
exposing flesh
naked in rawness
red with soreness.
Not looking but experiencing
the pain of powerlessness.

Síle Wall

Beauty

Beauty
arresting
enrapturing
engaging
compelling
penetrating
my whole person
heart and soul
mind and senses
Beauty
awaiting me everywhere
in
every human person
the petal of a flower
changing clouds
stream of sunlight
beam of moon
colours of sea
fall of snow
sweetness of birdsong
available only for those
who seek desire and hunger for it
in their heart

Begin Again

Each second I am reborn
each moment a new beginning
every day I begin again
something inside me
is always ready to say
yes
yes
yes
may I begin this day
knowing that nothing
can destroy the gift
of who I am

My Legacy

What is my legacy?
What will I leave behind?
Not what I have
stocks or shares
property or finance
rather who I am
Who I am
what I have been
and will be
is stamped into
all the lives I've touched
My
smiles
frowns
laughter
complaints
kindness
selfishness
My concern
for my family
and friends
and neighbours

*

(Continued)

My concern for
strangers
marginalized people
dispossessed people
migrants
and
refugees
for people who
are different from me
my care for the Earth
and for all beings
all are part of me
part of my legacy
that is equal
to the full potential
that is in me

To dare is to lose one's footing momentarily.
Not to dare is to lose oneself.

Søren Kierkegaard

These my elder years

May I see my elder years
as gift
a special time of life
Time
to be fully alive
to be full of life
to be full of love
to be full of God

May I see this time
not as about my age
or length of years
rather about living in
the values
offered to me
in this stage of life

May I be able to let go
of the life that I have planned
to live the life that awaits me

May I let go of the fantasies
of eternal youth
or fears of old age
to find the beauty
of what it means to age well

May I understand
this phase
as a new stage in life
May it enlighten me
and those around me

May I see life as a series of lives
each of them with its own
tasks
flavours
glories
possibilities
darknesses
and lights
all designed
to lead to fulfilment

(Continued)

May I see life as a mosaic
made up of many pieces
each of them
a stepping stone
to the next
each of them
having a particular purpose

May I see this time
as a time to sanctify time
to make it creative
rather than boring
A time to assimilate
all the other parts
and to become alive in ways
I have never been alive before

May I see this time
as a time to replace
old relationships with new ones
May I see it as a time
to be taken more slowly
reflectively
and more mindfully

May it be a time
to love more deeply
to laugh more heartily
to listen more carefully
A time not merely to be alive
but to be more fully alive
than ever before

May it be a time
when I welcome
all that is new
and encourage and affirm
the dreams and ideas
of the young

May it be a time
when I am comfortable
with the self that I am
not mourn what I am not

May it be a time
not to wallow in regrets
but to see them
as invitations

(Continued)

to revisit my ideals
urging me to be present
in a new way
in this new time

May I see it as a time
of continuous becoming.

Yesterday is but today's memory, and tomorrow is today's dream.

KAHLIL GIBRAN

The Meditation Session

Michael Harding

Sometimes I wake before dawn. Before anyone else is up. I lie there with a sense of gratefulness that I am still alive, and have slept so well and am still so warm and snug in my duvet.

I visit the bathroom. I brush my teeth and splash hot water on my face without putting on a single light, because the glow from my iPhone is soft and gently eases me into the day.

I take a jug from the shelf and fill it with well water that is kept in a bucket in the back kitchen.

Then I go outside. Sometimes the moon is in its first quarter. Sometimes it is full. And sometimes there is no moon at all. Just the stars. But I always stand for a moment to look at the moon. The well water is my offering. It symbolizes my heart. And I think of the billions of years this universe has been there waiting in all its emptiness for this moment. Waiting for me to come awake and be present to its vast authority.

That too makes me feel grateful. Just to be here. I feel naked in the timeless universe. And then I head onwards to my studio at the end of the garden.

I open the sliding glass door and go inside, taking off my shoes, crossing the floor in stocking feet, and holding the jug of water. I sit on a small cushion. I place the jug on the floor. And I become very still.

I feel a rush of gratefulness again for having survived the night. Though I know a night will come that I won't survive.

I light the candle. I pour the water into seven small waterbowls as an offering from my heart. I take charcoal from a container and hold it over the flame and then I spread incense on the charcoal. The flame illuminates the walls. I join my hands in front of me. I kneel and prostrate my body in a single movement. I stretch on the floor, feeling grateful for these clean floorboards.

Shadows dance on the walls. From the window comes the faint light of dawn as it seeps over the far mountain beyond the lake.

For a moment I am glad. And then the gladness dies. It dies like a flame going out. I see the glad man falling and the happy man lose his joy. My heart turns to stone. The room fills with disturbing emotions; all the stuff of yesterday, all the anxieties return. But they are no longer inside me, possessing me. They are in the room, all around me, flying in the air. I make a decision not to dance with them. They dance on their own. And I watch them die. Every emotion comes dancing, a line of them, from joy and gladness to anxiety and bitterness and jealousy and despair. They are like demons in the room – I can hear them scream. But I don't move. I just watch. Eventually they die.

I have destroyed them by simply being still, by simply breathing and remaining aware of my breathing. So a good feeling arises in me, a glow of contentment. The candlelight recovers the texture of a Christmas morning. It is gentle and warm and lovely. But I allow that loveliness to dance around the room until it too dies. And when all the loveliness is dead my muscles tense and the ugly thoughts in my heart, the dregs of my soul, rise and are retched up into the air.

There is no end to what is inside me. No end to the bile surfacing in me. And I allow it all without judging any of it. I don't pretend that the feelings of love and attachment are better than the feelings of hate. I acknowledge them all, the black and the white, as part of me.

The well water is the offering of my heart. But it triggers thoughts that distract me. The water makes me think of wine and song and all the parties of long ago, and the friends gathered at the table, chattering about their successes. I start dreaming of beautiful women singing, and old men slurring their words and young people perfumed and dressed for love. I have begun to doze. To drift into a fog of distractions. So I must begin the whole thing all over again.

I breathe.

I focus on the breath.

I remain still.

I observe what arises in my mind.

Each time I meditate I imagine my death that will come eventually like shadows creeping along the wall. And how sorrowful I will be then, crying for all the times I refused to love, and all the chances I lost and all the long life lived with my breath held and my heart closed. At other times in meditation I become angry, and it is like a fire in my gut. I burn. But I try to remain still even then, and to observe the fire, and allow the fire to burn out.

I used to think meditation sessions were tranquil. I was influenced by images of people with closed eyes and smiling faces and I got the impression that meditation was a calm and sweet affair; a pool of silence and repose that happy religious people dived into like children into a swimming pool. But it's not. It's fierce and disturbing. It is like the ocean. I see myself as I am: a contorted creature.

But if I sit for long enough I also see that my Self dissolves and withers. It burns down to nothing, until some presence in the room rises up and observes me.

It's like the quietness after a storm or the silence between the notes in a musical score. I rise and extinguish the candle. I pour water back from the vessels into the jug and I open the window and pour the water on to the rose bushes outside. I toss sand on the charcoal to quench the incense. I put on my shoes and go outside.

I am ready to return to the kitchen and join the others for breakfast. But I am not alone now. I am not lonely as I sit with the others. I am not frightened as I look to the future because there is a presence in the air around me now; a presence more real than myself. I don't know what it is, though I don't call it God or Buddha any more, because that would isolate me from the others. And I want to live with the others and share a good breakfast with them as we sit together at the table.

The Love of Christ urges us on

Caritas Christi urget nos

We all have an infinite capacity to love
placed in us by Love itself
The love which created me
is the greatest possible
unconditional love
which draws everyone
and everything to it
and to each other

This great gift of love urges me
to see the significance and goodness
and beauty of everyone
and everything

This great gift of love
urges me to overcome
my tendencies to exclude
those who are different from me

This great gift of love urges me
to appreciate the value
of what I see around me

This great gift of love urges me
to have a growing sense
of wonder and gratitude
for the way my life is blessed
by even the simplest things

This great gift of love urges me
To be in awe of God's presence
in the most ordinary of things.

This great gift of love urges me
to see the true value and significance
of each thing
and to be grateful for the gift it is

This great gift of love urges me
and frees me from being dominated
by my deficiencies and
to see what is positive
in myself and others

(Continued)

This great gift of love urges me
to seek out
the poor
the sick
the lonely
the marginalized
and the excluded people
and bring them solace

As this great gift of love frees me
to see all
in Christ
in its radiant light
everyone and everything
no matter how insignificant
becoming a sign of love
joy
praise
and
gratitude

Unknown

The not knowing path
Winds under and over
In and out
A gentling reaching out
Touching other paths
Unknown and known
Encountering in touch
Feelings once known
Now unknown

Síle Wall

*Let us always meet each other with a smile,
for the smile is the beginning of love.*

MOTHER TERESA

speak to you . . .

I speak to you in the life of every breath you take
Be still and know that I am

I speak to you as you breathe in and breathe out
Be still and know that I am

I speak to you in the sound of silence
Be still and know that I am

I speak to you in all of creation
Be still and know that I am

I speak to you in the sunlight that wakes you in the day
Be still and know that I am

I speak to you in the colours that set the sun
Be still and know that I am

I speak to you in the moonlight when the moon is full
Be still and know that I am

(Continued)

I speak to you in the whisper of moonlight in the water
Be still and know that I am

I speak to you in the moonlight as the moon wanes
Be still and know that I am

I speak to you in the darkness of the pregnant clouds
Be still and know that I am

I speak to you in the snow falling gently on the slate roofs
Be still and know that I am

I speak to you in the abundance of the Earth
Be still and know that I am

I speak to you in the freshness of the verdant grass
Be still and know that I am

I speak to you in the glistening of the morning dew
Be still and know that I am

I speak to you in the fragrance of new mown hay
Be still and know that I am

I speak to you in every ear of corn
Be still and know that I am

I speak to you in the stem of every flower
Be still and know that I am

I speak to you in the budding of every snowdrop
Be still and know that I am

I speak to you in the beauty of every blossom
Be still and know that I am

I speak to you in the fragility of every petal
Be still and know that I am

I speak to you in the greenly spirit of every tree
Be still and know that I am

I speak to you in the uniqueness of every branch
Be still and know that I am

I speak to you in the design of every leaf
Be still and know that I am

(Continued)

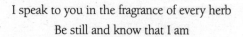

I speak to you in the fragrance of every herb
Be still and know that I am

I speak to you in the darkness of a raging storm
Be still and know that I am

I speak to you in the beauty of a deep blue sky
Be still and know that I am

I speak to you in the colours of an autumn evening
Be still and know that I am

I speak to you in the singing of a feather in a summer breeze
Be still and know that I am

I speak to you in the rain that caresses my face
Be still and know that I am

I speak to you in the wind that blows through my hair
Be still and know that I am

I speak to you in the stability of every mountain
Be still and know that I am

I speak to you in the sound of water flowing
Be still and know that I am

I speak to you in the gurgling of every stream
Be still and know that I am

I speak to you in the waves gently lapping
Be still and know that I am

I speak to you in the storm's crashing waves
Be still and know that I am

I speak to you in every grain of sand on the seashore
Be still and know that I am

I speak to you in the flutter of birds' wings on high
Be still and know that I am

I speak to you in the song of every bird that sings
Be still and know that I am

I speak to you in every cuckoo announcing the summer
Be still and know that I am

(Continued)

I speak to you in every gull calling the rain
Be still and know that I am

I speak to you in the natural beauty of woodland
Be still and know that I am

I speak to you in all that is human
Be still and know that I am

I speak to you through distant bells calling
Be still and know that I am

I speak to you in all the churches, mosques, temples
and synagogues
Be still and know that I am

I speak to you in the preachers and pastors
Be still and know that I am

I speak to you in the deepest core of your being
Be still and know that I am

I speak to you in the richness of humanity
Be still and know that I am

I speak to you in the fragility of human nature
Be still and know that I am

I speak to you in the generosity of every parent
Be still and know that I am

I speak to you in the beat of every broken heart
Be still and know that I am

I speak to you in the hope that has set your heart free
Be still and know that I am

I speak to you in the love you find in another's eyes
Be still and know that I am

I speak to you in the trust of every infant's step
Be still and know that I am

I speak to you in the laughter of every child
Be still and know that I am

I speak to you in every voice for justice
Be still and know that I am

(Continued)

I speak to you in every cry for love
Be still and know that I am

I speak to you in every beggar on the street
Be still and know that I am

I speak to you in the hand that helps you
Be still and know that I am

I speak to you in the hope you hold on to when
darkness comes
Be still and know that I am

I speak to you in all your heart is yearning
Be still and know that I am

I speak to you in all your heart desires
Be still and know that I am

I speak to you in all that is natural
Be still and know that I am

I speak to you in all that is infinite
Be still and know that I am

I speak to you in all that is finite
Be still and know that I am

I speak to you in all that is yes
Be still and know that I am

Love feels no burden, thinks nothing of trouble, attempts what is above its strength, pleads no excuse of impossibility; for it thinks all things lawful for itself, and all things possible.

THOMAS À KEMPIS

This Moment

A neighbourhood.
At dusk.

Things are getting ready
to happen
out of sight.

Stars and moths.
And rinds slanting around fruit.

But not yet.

One tree is black.
One window is yellow as butter.

A woman leans down to catch a child
who has run into her arms
this moment.

Stars rise.
Moths flutter.
Apples sweeten in the dark.

Eavan Boland

Contributors

to *Seasons of Hope*

EAVAN BOLAND has been Writer in Residence at Trinity College and University College, Dublin. She was poet in residence at the National Maternity Hospital during its Centenary in 1994, and was the Hurst Professor at Washington University and Regent's Lecturer at the University of California. She currently teaches at Stanford University, where she is Mabury/Knapp Professor in the Humanities Department and Director of the Creative Writing Programme. She is also on the board of the Irish Arts Council, a member of the Irish Academy of Letters and is on the advisory board of the International Writers' Center at Washington University. She has published ten volumes of poetry and received the Lannan Award for Poetry and an American Ireland Fund Literary Award.

THEO DORGAN is a poet, novelist, prose writer, screenwriter, editor and translator. Among his recent works are *Time on the Ocean: A Voyage from Cape Horn to Cape Town*, the novel *Making Way*, the collection of poems *Greek*, the libretto *Jason and the Argonauts* and a collection of essays he edited, *Foundation Stone: Notes towards a Constitution for a 21st Century Republic*. A new collection of poems is forthcoming in late 2014. He is a member of Aosdána.

MICHAEL HARDING is the author of the bestselling, award-winning *Staring at Lakes*. He writes a weekly creative chronicle of Irish midland life for the *Irish Times* but is best known as a playwright of such plays as *Strawboys, Una Pooka, Misogynist, Hubert Murray's Widow, Sour Grapes* and *Amazing Grace*, all produced by the Abbey Theatre, and more than a dozen other plays for leading Irish companies. He has also written three novels, *Priest, The Trouble With Sarah Gullion*, and *Bird in the Snow* and is a member of Aosdána.

RUAIRÍ MCKIERNAN is an award-winning social innovator and campaigner. He is the founder of the SpunOut.ie youth organization, a co-founder of Uplift, a people-powered campaigning organization, and a member of the Council of State.

SEÁN MCDONAGH was ordained in 1969 and was assigned to work in the Philippines, where he taught anthropology and linguistics. In 1994 he was appointed as international coordinator for Justice, Peace and the Integrity of Creation for the Columban Missionaries Society. He has written ten books and numerous articles relating to justice, peace and ecology. His first book *To Care for the Earth* was one of the first books on ecotheology published in English. His most recent book is *Fukushima: The Death Knell for Nuclear Energy?*

FR. PETER MCVERRY, SJ was ordained as a Jesuit Priest in 1975. While working as a priest in inner-city Dublin he encountered some homeless children and opened a hostel for them in 1979. He subsequently opened twelve hostels, a residential drug-detox centre, two drug-free after-care houses, a residential drug stabilization centre and about ninety apartments for long-term accommodation needs. Peter's campaigning for, and involvement with, troubled young people has made him one of the most prophetic voices in Ireland today. The organization he started was called the Arrupe Society but was renamed several years ago as the Peter McVerry Trust. He has written on many issues relating to young homeless people, such as accommodation, drugs, juvenile justice, the gardai, prisons and education. In 2003, he produced a book of his writings, *The Meaning is in the Shadows*. His most recent publication is *Jesus – Social Revolutionary?*

KORKO MOSES, SJ is a Jesuit priest from India who founded Dhyana Vanam Ashram in Dindigul, Southern India, an ashram inspired by both Christian and Eastern spiritual traditions. He is a spiritual guide, counsellor, a teacher of meditation and yoga, and leads retreats regularly. He has worked with people with addictions and also offers spiritual guidance for the L'Arche communities.

SISTER THÉRÈSE MURPHY was, until recently, Abbess of the Poor Clare Convent, Ennis. She was born in Scotland of Irish parents and grew up in northern Rhodesia/Zambia. Educated by the Notre Dame sisters in South Africa, she worked in Barclays Bank before joining the Poor Clare Sisters in Ennis in 1961. She believes passionately in the contemplative life and in its irreplaceable contribution to our world.

SISTER STAN is a well-known social activist, campaigner and founder of a number of voluntary organizations, including Focus Ireland, the Immigrant Council of Ireland, Young Social Innovators and the Sanctuary. She is the author of several books, including *The Road Home: A Memoir*, *Stillness*, *Moments of Stillness*, *Gardening the Soul* and the bestselling *Day by Day*. She lives and works in Dublin.

SÍLE WALL is a Religious Sister of Charity with many years' experience of working in the voluntary sector with a particular emphasis on issues related to mental health, learning disability and homelessness. She has been involved in the development of the Sanctuary, Dublin, since it was founded in 1998 and currently practises there as an art therapist as well as leading meditation/mindfulness practices and workshops.

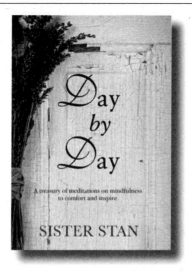

Day by Day
Sister Stan

SISTER STAN's *Day by Day* offers words of wisdom that will inspire and comfort you on your journey through life. Thoughtful and reflective, it draws upon some of the most enlightened figures from both the past and the present as it gently guides you through your day.

Also included are thought-provoking contributions on a range of subjects, including mindfulness, gratitude, belonging, friendship and courage, from influential figures such as Abbot Mark Patrick Hederman, psychologist and founder of Headstrong, Dr Tony Bates, poet Brendan Kennelly, and producer/director Lelia Doolan, each helping Sister Stan to create an invaluable treasury for our times.

Published by Transworld Ireland
978-184827166-1
£12.99